How to **Act** & **Eat** at the **Same Time**

A book by
TOM LOGAN

with a Foreword by
Marc Hirschfeld
Executive Vice President,
Casting, NBC Entertainment

How to **Act** & **Eat**
at the Same Time

THE SEQUEL

The Do's and Don'ts of Landing a Professional Acting Job

Limelight Editions
512 Newark Pompton Turnpike
Pompton Plains, New Jersey 07444

First published in 2004 by Limelight Editions
Reprinted in 2006

Printed in the United States of America

Book design by Rachel Reiss

Library of Congress Cataloging-in-Publication Data

Logan, Tom, 1953-
   How to act and eat at the same time : the sequel / Tom
Logan.—1st Limelight ed.
      p. cm.
   ISBN 978-0-87910-991-2
   1. Acting—Vocational guidance. I. Title: How to act & eat at
the same time. II. Title.

PN2055.L64 2003
792.02'8'023—dc22

                                        2003019295

www.limelighteditions.com

This book is dedicated to two of the most wonderful, loving, thoughtful and caring people on the planet Earth (or any other planet for that matter); my two sons, Lear and Baron. You are the absolute joy of my life. "Daddo" loves you more than anything in the whole wide world.

Acknowledgments

Grateful acknowledgment is made to the staff of the Screen Actors Guild, Christopher Eid and David Lotz of Actors' Equity Association, and Jayne Wallace, Aimee Phillips, and Megan Capuano of the American Federation of Television and Radio Artists. Acknowledgment is also made to these unions for permission to reprint the material used in the Appendices, and to the following actors for permission to reprint their photographs: Kevin Cater, Cheyenne Overall, and Charlie Scola; to Keith and Kevin Schultz of Schultz Bros. Photography; and to Nina Maynard for her detailed editorial expertise. Thanks to Rachel Reiss for her very creative interior and cover designs.

A special acknowledgment is made to the publisher, Mel Zerman, for his hard work, dedication, support, friendship, and especially for the literary freedom to write this book in my own style.

Contents

Foreword

"Auditioning has absolutely nothing to do with acting." That's the headline. Many actors spend years toiling away in this business without figuring that out.

During the course of my long career as a casting director and network executive I have witnessed some of the finest actors in Hollywood "crash and burn" during an audition because of weak audition skills. Years of training at Juilliard, NYU, Northwestern, and Yale hone your skills at acting, but not at audition technique. And unless you figure out the difference between the two, you'll never make it from the casting director's office to the set of a television series or feature film.

As an actor, you are required to make so many decisions during the audition process that will never be asked of you again once you actually book the role. For instance, you have to be your own wardrobe person and director prior to an audition, many times without the benefit of reading a full script. Most actors are only given access to a short audition scene (also referred to as "sides") for the purposes of the audition and from two or three pages of dialogue must create their multidimensional character. This is a Herculean task. You also need to separate yourself from the rest of the "pack." How do you make your audition distinctive, unique and memorable (in a positive way!) from dozens of other actors auditioning for the same role?

Tom Logan's book is a comprehensive guide to the art of the audition and I recommend it without hesitation. Many of the examples he gives, illustrating gaffes and blunders that actors make during the audition process, are eerily similar to the ones I've seen dozens of times during my tenure in the casting profession. Study this guide and don't make the same mistakes that are made every day by actors who audition and never book the role. Remember, once you have studied and learned the basic tools of acting....

Acting is easy. Auditioning is hard.

Marc Hirschfeld
Executive Vice President, Casting
NBC Entertainment

Marc Hirschfeld is one of the most highly regarded casting directors in Los Angeles and New York. Before becoming head of casting for the NBC network, Mr. Hirschfeld cast many top TV series and films including *Seinfeld, Third Rock From the Sun, The Larry Sanders Show, Grace Under Fire, The Wonder Years, Party of Five, Married....with Children, The Drew Carey Show, X-Files: The Movie,* and won an Emmy for casting "From the Earth to the Moon" miniseries on HBO.

Preface

Recently I was on an airplane from Los Angeles to New York, begging for a bag of peanuts, which I spent the next five minutes trying to pry open. Then I noticed that the woman sitting next to me was reading the original version of my book, *How to Act and Eat at the Same Time.*

I said to her, "Oh, excuse me, but I read that book and found it to be incomplete and not very well-written." She turned to me tersely and said, "I disagree. It has been very helpful and I'm reading it for the second time."

"Yeah, maybe," I quipped, "but there are much better books out there on the subject." She replied, "Oh, well, whatever . . . . I like it." "To each his own," I said.

A few moments later she looked me right in the eye, opened the book to the picture of the author on the inside cover and said matter-of-factly, "The author, Tom Logan, happens to be a very close, personal friend of mine and I don't think he'd appreciate you saying that."

I was stunned, but asked, "Does he look like this picture?" "Exactly," she stated.

That photo of me was taken when the Bible was a twenty-page scroll and the Dead Sea wasn't even sick yet. It was during this conversation that I decided to expand and update *How to Act and Eat at the Same Time* into a sequel.

When I had written the original book fourteen years before the airplane confrontation, I hadn't directed any feature films, television shows, or commercials; I was a very-working actor. Now being on the other side of casting has given me a whole different perspective.

In this update you will hear about the profession of acting from both sides of the camera; from a previously working actor's to a now working TV, film, and commercial director's perspective, who also writes and produces.

I have added eight chapters and performed major changes and updates to the original eight chapters. To that woman on the airplane, wherever you are, I thank you.

Introduction

Please do me a favor: Don't read this book with false expectations. I'm not going to tell you who's sleeping with whom, or who's having whose baby. Nor am I going to tell you how, in just ten easy steps, actors (herein used to designate both genders) have attained stardom overnight. If you're interested in such stories, then read some of the popular magazines and tabloids that you can pick up at your local supermarket checkout.

I just hope you don't put much faith in those publications. Keep in mind that they interview people who have been taken aboard spaceships, people with intellectual bypasses who have been reincarnated from some animal, and fly-by-night doctors who prescribe astrology for birth control. My book contains no such stories.

This is not a where-to or a how-to book: where to live in Los Angeles or New York, how to find an apartment, where to get the best answering service, how to manage your money, how to find a job as a waiter, where to obtain a massage, how to "get into character" (e.g., "crawling around on the floor acting like a lion"), where to get the best health foods, how to find a good therapist, how to share the experiences of yoga and meditation, how to talk to your inner self, or how to deal with astrological problems associated with your "moon" being in Cincinnati. And I'm not going to discuss the Strasberg Method, the Stanislavsky Method, or the Rhythm Method. Plenty of excellent books cover the above subjects very well; you should read all of them.

My expertise is telling you how to get the job in the first place and I'm devoting all of these pages to that and that alone. Much of the information in the first eight chapters is information you are incredibly unlikely to have experienced, unless you've sat in auditions day after day as a director or casting director.

If you have read many of the books that are on the market about how to get into the acting business, you will have seen some differing opinions. One of the main reasons for these differences is, show business is not a science. Another is the slant of each book depends on what area of the acting business happens to be of the author's expertise. Some of the books on this subject are written by actors, some by agents, others by casting directors or attorneys or theatre people, and so on. The backgrounds of some of the industry professionals who wrote those books may be heavier in commercials than in feature films, and vice versa. Some might have experience dealing with sitcoms, while others might work on episodic, dramatic television.

Although my particular specialty is directing feature films, I have also directed many commercials and numerous episodic TV shows, as well as writing and producing for the same mediums.

Before becoming a full-time screen director, I made my complete living as an actor for many, many years, performing first in over seventy professional live stage productions from New York to Los Angeles and then as an actor with starring roles in soap operas, episodic television, commercials, and feature films. It is my behind-the-camera experience that I will combine with the front-of-the-camera experience as I write about how to get into the acting profession.

SHOW BUSINESS is two words—SHOW and BUSINESS. And you know what? The word "Business" is longer than the word "Show." Acting is a business with its own world. Make no mistake about that. It is easy to get "ripped off" when pursuing a professional acting career. Actors are ripped off every day, every hour, and every minute. How do I know this happens? Well, I've encountered plenty of rogues who make their living off actors like you, who don't know how to go about starting a legitimate acting career. There is so much misinformation with regards to this business. Smart is when you believe half of what you hear; brilliant is when you know which half. By the time you finish this book, you will know which half.

I will help you to stay ahead of the con artists. Believe me, they're out there and they'll put the screws on you faster than an undertaker. Don't picture underworld figures or Mafia types. These characters have white houses with white picket fences and SUVs. They will give you all kinds of promises for success and try to take money from you. After reading this book, however, you will have no doubt whom you should give money to, when to give, and for what purposes. You'll reveal these cheats, like pulling the curtain back on the great and powerful Oz.

Spending time with some industry people will have you believing that man's descent from the ape hasn't started yet. It even becomes apparent that there are more believable characters on *Star Trek* than there are in show business. Do I fault the con artist apes? Absolutely! But the real fault lies with actors who are so starstruck that they fall for a lot of the get-rich schemes in which only the cons get rich. These con artists know that there are no easy ways to make it as an actor. Plow ahead with good business sense and forget the promises that people will make. It may not be easy, but you can ACT AND EAT AT THE SAME TIME.

For the past fifteen years in every audition I've held, I have written down every comment made about each actor. Every night I log all of those comments into a computer. I have been doing this since 1988. For a major commercial audition, I could see two hundred actors in a day, because unlike most directors, I like to personally meet every actor who auditions. Eight people might be in the room watching the playbacks; if each person made only one comment (I wish!) about each actor, that would amount to sixteen hundred comments in one day alone.

Every six months I go into that computer and pull out the data. Compiling and analyzing the data resulted in consistent and astounding information from year to year. For instance, we cast someone wearing blue, aqua, or turquoise 69.1 percent of the time. From a two-person audition scene we rarely cast you with the person you actually read with; 71.3 percent of the time we cast the person on the right side of the screen. By logging the exact time the person we cast actually auditioned, I discovered the best time to audition is 1:18 P.M.!

On the basis of the information I collected, you're going to reap the benefits in this book. If I wrote about what *I* liked and disliked about actors—BIG DEAL. That would give you some limited help, if you were auditioning for me only. But I intend to explain what "the industry" likes and dislikes about actors based upon thousands of directors', casting directors', and producers' comments, taken right from actual film, television, and commercial auditions. I believe this is the one thing that separates my book from others on this subject. However, as previously mentioned, I believe you should read every book, and I mean every book, on this subject to broaden your knowledge. All of them have a lot to offer.

Since many of you are already going on auditions, the first half of this book deals with the "Don'ts" of auditioning. The second half is devoted to getting into an audition in the first place. To some this may seem backwards. After all, if you're just starting out you have a lot of work to do before you go on your first audition. But many of you are already auditioning and probably making the mistakes you're going to read about in the first eight chapters. So, I want to stop this type of behavior before it goes on any further.

For those of you just starting out, I want to get this information to you before you enter your first audition, so you won't start off on the wrong foot. Hopefully you beginners will learn what not to do first! If I can get this information to you early enough, you won't develop the bad habits detrimental to your career.

I'm writing this book from my heart with you, the actor, in my mind. After all, it is you, the actor, who will make me, the director, look good or bad. But be forewarned. This book will tell you how it is, not how it should be. I wish us all the best of luck.

PART ONE
The Don'ts

CHAPTER ONE

Don't Apologize

One day I was auditioning actors for a feature film that I was directing at Universal Studios. Since we were holding final callbacks, there were about eight people in the room for each actor to meet. Before the first actor arrived, one of the producers put a dollar bill into a paper cup and said, "Put me down for four."

He then passed the cup to another producer who added his dollar and said, "Put me down for six." The cup passed to me. I had no idea what the clowns were doing, but since they were responsible for my paycheck, I played along.

"Put me down for eight," I proudly announced and put in a dollar. The cup went around to all eight people. Each played the game as though they understood what it was all about. In retrospect, they all did understand, but at the time I didn't.

It was after the first actor left the room that I figured out what the game was. It is so common that actors apologize, so common that they feel the need to tell us how incompetent they are, so common that they want to point out all of their mistakes, and so common that they want to tell how much better they normally do, that these guys were taking bets on how many times each actor would apologize!

At a major studio with well-known actors who should have known better, I won one hundred-and-ninety-seven dollars that day! I quickly learned how to play the game: always pick the highest number. That day, after each actor left the room we spent more time arguing over what constituted an apology than we did on the actors' performances. Sad, but very true.

Apologizing is the number one complaint about you in auditions according to my previously mentioned extensive research. It's not the number one complaint about your performance, but it is the number one complaint about you personally and has remained the number one complaint year after year. Apologizing has never fallen to number two. Having said all of the above, if you spill coffee on someone in the audition room, then by all means apologize. I'm talking about apologizing for your performance or anything related to it.

Who Actually Casts the Show?

Before we go into extensive detail about why and how actors apologize, we must first discuss why they should not apologize. To do this we must determine who actually casts the show. Basically, projects are being cast by people who probably know less about acting than you do! Which creates a problem for you when you walk into an audition and everyone tells you what they're looking for.

We all contradict ourselves. The producer is looking for someone he can date. The director is hopefully looking for someone who can act (although, sometimes you wonder). The writer, on heavy medication and living in a purple haze since the '60s listening to Innagottadavita for the last sixteen hours, has inhaled too many bus fumes, and has eaten too many paint chips. Okay, I jest to make the point that everyone in the room is not an expert on acting and everyone has their own agenda. So to whom should you really listen?

Let's say you're auditioning for a show to be aired on NBC. Everyone in the room says a few words about the character for which you're auditioning, but who actually has the power in the room? "NBC," you answer. Well, yes, when it comes to the top few roles, such as series regulars, the top starring role(s) in a movie for television, or a network pilot, then the network executives in that department do have control. The top few starring roles may need to get "network approval." But who really casts all the other parts, the ones for which you'll most likely be reading?

"The producer," you chime in. Do you know which producer? Let's see now . . . . there's the Producer(s), the Co-Producer(s), the Executive Producer(s), the Co-Executive Producer(s), the Line Producer(s), the Coordinating Producer(s), the Consulting Producer(s), the Supervising Producer(s), the Segment Producer(s), the Associate Producer(s), the Assistant Producer(s), and so forth.

Many times I've watched shows on TV or films in the theatre that I've directed and looked at all the producer credits and realized that I've never met half these people! Sometimes I think a bunch of names are added on the screen to make the show look a lot more impressive than it really is. Many times it's the father-in-law, the brother-in-law, or the son-in-law, of someone important. Maybe it's a Lewinsky thing.

Yes, the top producers do have their say, and they are extremely important people when it comes to casting, especially in episodic television versus feature films. And sometimes, depending on the various relationships of the people involved, they do make some, even many, final casting decisions.

One of the first things you learn when you arrive in Los Angeles or New York is that everyone calls themselves a producer. You don't have to have produced anything to call yourself a producer. You just tell people that you are "in development" of a particular script and they'll think you are producing. "In development" is taken to mean that no one wants your script yet. Everyone owns a script, usually one they wrote themselves or have thought about writing, and that alone seems to qualify one as a producer. Merely having dreamed of producing seems to qualify you to use the title.

To be a producer is great for the social life. Business cards printed up with your name and producer title on them really make you look impressive. I refer to these people as "fake producers," of whom there are two types: Those who think they are God and those who are certain of it. The bottom line is that of all these "wanna-bes" very few, and I mean an incredibly small minority, have ever actually produced anything. Being such a producer is like running a cemetery—you have a lot of people under you, but none of them are listening. Real produc-ers, however, are generally very nice, intelligent, and respectable people.

You proudly announce, "The casting director casts the show." Casting directors do not cast and they do not direct the show. Yes, they do "direct the casting," but don't confuse this with the one who casts the show. Confusing? We're not really sure where the term "cast-ing director" comes from. In fact, the next time you're viewing a film or television show look for the words "casting director" on the screen. You're very unlikely to see them.

There's a reason the title of "director" is not attached to the person who is holding the auditions. According to the "Basic Agreement" with producers and production companies from the Directors Guild of America, in paragraph 8-103, only two positions can actually use the term "director" in their title; the actual director and his assistants, known as assistant directors. Because of pre-existing agreements with other unions, the Directors Guild does permit two other people to use the term director in their title: "art director" and "director of pho-tography." As far as "director" credits are concerned, that's it.

You'll see "casting" and then a name, or you'll see "casting by . . . . ," but not "casting director." Off the record, everyone including directors calls them "casting directors."

In no way does this play down their importance. To the contrary, casting directors have an extremely important job that is invaluable to the casting process. We can't function without them. They weed out thousands of actors, narrowing the field down to the few who will meet with the people who do make final decisions. So, a casting di-rector usually can't say "yes" to you, but as important, she can say "no."

The casting director is absolutely the actor's best friend, the one who fights for you in an audition. Many a time a casting director has changed the mind of the powers that be who weren't going to cast a particular actor. It has happened many times that an actor didn't do a very good reading, but the casting director found some piece of film on the actor from another project, showed it to the right people, and all of a sudden that actor had a job. Never discount the importance of the casting director. *Never!*

But we're still back to the original question: Who actually casts the show?

"The writer," you ask? Unless the writer has other functions, the writer hardly ever sees an actor in an audition. Writers, especially in episodic television, do have some say, depending on who they are and whether or not they are also the producers. In situation-comedy, if the writer is also the producer he has a lot of clout and may have final say. However, with the exception of the above cases, the writer doesn't cast the show.

I mentioned that the first thing you learn when you arrive in Los Angeles or New York is that everyone is a producer. The second thing you learn is that everyone is a writer. For extra attention many people claim to be writer/producers. Again, you don't have to have written anything to call yourself a writer, as long as you have thought about writing something at some point in your life. If an idea has ever crossed your mind, then most people who don't know any better will consider you a writer. Again, of all the people claiming to be writers, an incredibly small number have ever written anything, and even fewer have ever had anything actually produced.

So unless he's a sitcom writer and producer, he will have practically no input in casting. I've directed feature films where I didn't even meet the writer until the end of the shoot. Unless the writer is wearing more than one hat (i.e., producer), ironically he has even less power over script changes to his own script than does the director and producer.

Okay, now you're having to think. "The director," you might concede. The third lesson for Los Angeles and New York arrivals is that everyone wants to direct, although directing is harder to fake because everyone wants to know what you've actually directed. Anyone who has ever directed a play in any theatre anywhere in the world likes to call himself a director. As with writers and producers, even if people like to be referred to as a director, most haven't directed anything on screen.

If you guess that the director casts the show, you're going to win the washer-dryer combination. With the exception of episodic and sitcom TV, which many times are "cast by committee," you would usually be correct. I, as the director, am normally going to cast my own shows, especially feature films. It stands to reason that since the director is responsible for the actors' performances, he should make those decisions.

I say "usually" because there are other people who might have final say. For instance, if a movie-of-the-week is being sponsored by Burger King, then the director might have to have casting discussions with the Burger King people since they are paying for it. Remember the phrase "Show me the money," from the film, *Jerry Maguire*? In other words, the people who *can* have the final say may know nothing about acting.

The casting by committee method often used for episodic television is complicated. It could involve the director, and/or producer, and/or writer/producers, and/or network executives, and/or the sponsors, or any combination of these. In other words, who knows with any particular episodic TV show who has the power?

On the other hand, let's say you're auditioning for a feature film. Then 99 percent of the time the director is going to have final say. But, still, it gets down to "Show me the money." Whoever is paying, rules, and that person is frequently sporting a business suit and understands nothing about what you are doing in that audition.

Many directors refer to the above people as "suits." Basically, a "suit" is someone who wears a coat and tie, has power over my life, and generally ticks me off. I say this somewhat in jest, since as a rule we work very well together; but when you hear the term "suit" in show business, you'll know to whom the director is referring.

Casting for the commercial you are auditioning for asks the same question. Yes, usually the director has a lot of say. But the people who *can*, and many times *do* have all final say are representatives from the product (i.e., account executives from the ad agency). They may be specialists in marketing the best hamburgers on earth, but not necessarily specialists in the audition process.

Even when the director does cast the show or has a major hand in it, don't assume he's an expert with actors either. Most actors who have been in stage plays are used to the director spending his time with them developing their characters, etc., and have a total misconception of what screen directors do. Stage directors have a few things to worry about other than the actors, but not nearly to the extent that a screen director has.

A screen director has to really understand all phases of filmmaking. He has to hire hundreds of crew members who have to work together like an oiled machine. He has to understand editing so completely as to be able to shoot a show that can actually be edited. A director has to work out in advance how he's going to shoot the show so that when it goes to the editing room it will piece together. He has to understand the camera and what effect each length of lens has on the total effect of the show. He has to understand lighting and what types of lights to use in all kinds of different situations. He has to keep the cast and crew (both with substantial egos) happy during impossible shooting situations and time frames. He has to understand wardrobe and how patterns in clothes affect the look of the show, and on, and on, and on.

For the reasons mentioned above, and a million more, the director's total focus isn't just on the actors. I hope I don't act like a traffic cop, but many directors do: "Walk over here, stare to the right of camera, then walk to your left, out of frame." Once you have been cast, don't look for a screen director to spend too much time talking about your character's motivations. It's great if you get lucky enough to work with a screen director who understands much about acting, but don't automatically count on it.

At an audition, it comes down to this: When you walk in the door, many times the suits and others have no idea what you're about to do; while you're doing it many have no idea what you're doing; and when you're finished some have no idea what you just did. In other words, many of those who are judging you could collectively be down to 20 brain cells in acting comprehension. Some of their brain scans would be a still-life. It's just a fact that their cage wheel may be turning but the hamster's dead. It's hard to describe the atmosphere among the suits in an audition, but the barroom scene in *Star Wars* comes close.

Because some people in the audition room may not be the sharpest knife in the drawer, it doesn't mean you should avoid acting classes. No! No! No! Olympic athletes are the best in their fields because they practice day after day to become the best at their craft. And so should you.

You should realize that once you start studying acting you will become the expert in the audition room, not us. Whether that's true, and I believe it is, you must believe it fully to give successful auditions. (Look at Chapter Eight for more on the importance of training.)

Acting is the only profession where people want to tell potential employers how incompetent they are when trying to get a job from us, when many of "us" could be as incompetent. No other profession does this. Before an operation, the doctor doesn't stand at the door to the operating room and explain that he hasn't done this very often and is extremely nervous. He doesn't say "oops" in the middle of an operation. Nor does the pilot stand at the door as passengers board and apologize about his upcoming performance with regards to their flight. But every actor apologizes in an audition. I take that back.... What actors do is worse, because the surgeon and airline pilot already have their jobs! They're not auditioning for work. The actor doesn't have the job yet and he's already apologizing for his performance!

The Many Ways Actors Apologize

Now, let's discuss the many ways actors apologize. I can tell you what you're going to do the minute you walk in the door—apologize. The apology will go something like this, "Well, ah, the reason I was late and everything is because my car broke down and then

I had to call the AAA, and then the AAA had a flat tire and their muf-fler blew up.... "

Number one: We don't care. Number two: We don't care. Number three: We don't care. Number four: Who cares? Once you actually come into the audition room with the director, I doubt he even knows that you're late. We don't have timecards. And even if we did, we would assume you were late because the casting director paired you with someone other than she originally thought.

Having said this *does not give you permission to be late!* Absolutely not. If you're late, you will have to answer to the casting director, who won't look favorably on you for the next audition. Lateness really angers casting directors, as it should. If some road-rage, L.A. type per-son cut you off on the freeway and you're late, don't apologize in the actual audition room with the director. Tell the secretary who checks you in that you are sorry—if she stares at you.

Would you like it if I was a house painter and arrived at your house late and then said something to the effect of "You know, the reason I'm late and everything is 'cos my truck broke down and I didn't have the money to have it towed and.... "?

Lateness at the end of the day might not even allow you an apol-ogy. It could spell disaster for your audition. Showing up at 5:00 P.M. for a 4:30 P.M. appointment may not get you an audition at all. The producer and director have probably already left, with the audition tape dubbed and ready to be sent off to the suits.

On the subject of timing, don't go into the actual audition room until you are ready. You score no points for volunteering to go in early or be-fore you feel comfortable with the script. After all, no one in the audi-tion room knows that you are being "Mr. Nice Guy" and volunteering. They have no idea how long you've been in the lobby working on that script. However, don't take this to the extreme. If you are reading for a sixty-year-old man and you were a teenager when you arrived....

Don't arrive at the audition just on time. Be there *before* your call time. If we're on schedule and you have arrived at the exact time you're supposed to, you might be called into the audition room immediately with little, or no, "down time." Arriving fifteen minutes early is cutting it a little close, but acceptable. I suggest you arrive about thirty minutes early. If you know about the audition the day before and have never been to the address, it might behoove you to drive over there beforehand and make sure you can find it before you start your actual journey the next day.

Another reason for arriving early to an audition is to help you relieve stress. Traffic in Los Angeles, for instance, is atrocious. And parking isn't much better. Yes, Screen Actors Guild (an organization we'll discuss in more detail throughout this book) guidelines state that we must provide parking for auditioning actors. Hopefully, everyone follows the rules. Either way, if you arrive late and rush into an audition, you are not helping yourself to relax before your reading.

If we are running a few minutes behind, don't complain. Sometimes we get behind schedule and often through no fault of the people in the room. And if it is our fault, it might be to your advantage. One reason I'm behind schedule may be because I'm giving each actor more time than the casting director allowed. Believe me, we want to get out of that audition faster than you do. We've been there all day, seeing and hearing the same lines delivered hundreds of times. So however frustrated you are with us for being late, we're more frustrated about it. We could catch up by giving some actors less time and by rushing them, but this isn't to your benefit.

Another apology many actors make is something like, "You know, I'm kind of nervous . . . . I haven't done this very much." I've even had actors who are well-known and had starring credits start apologizing in this way. Conversely, I've had other actors who have done "diddly squat" make their community theatre play sound as though it was *Gone with the Wind*. Apparently it isn't obvious to most actors, but the latter is the much better position to take.

The next apology will go something like this: "Well, Tom, ah, I just got here a few minutes ago and I haven't had a lot of time to look over the script and I'm kind of unprepared." Here you are walking into a room full of people who have no idea what you're about to do and you're telling them how poorly you're about to do it!

How would you like it if that painter who shows up at your house says, "You know, I just got here a few minutes ago and I haven't had a lot of time to mix the paints, so I'm a little unprepared to paint your house right now"? Would this give you a good feeling about the work he's about to do?

There is almost no excuse for being unprepared in an audition. *Being unprepared is actually the number one gripe about you* in an audition. As I don't have enough material to write an entire chapter on it, I'm including it in this chapter since it is part of apologizing.

According to the Screen Actors Guild guidelines we are supposed to make the script or sides (the few pages from the script) available in advance to all auditioning actors. If your agent can't get hold of the material, it is perfectly acceptable for you to phone the casting director's office and ask to see a copy of the script. If it's a feature film project, the odds are that very few actors will get to see a full script. Even so, you can phone the casting director's office and ask one of the assistants if you can come by the office and read a full script. If that doesn't work, phone the production company and see if they'll let you read the script before you are to audition. There are even websites (discussed later) that might have portions of the script available.

And if you are unprepared (shame on you!), don't try to make it look as though it's the casting director's fault. No, it's almost always the actor's fault. If you try to imply that it was the casting director's fault she probably will never call you in to another audition. You want to make the casting director look good, not blame her!

Don't qualify your excuse for being unprepared by saying you have three other auditions that same day. We, also, have a million other things going on that day and we're prepared for the audition. When you use this excuse, you make our audition seem less important to you.

Even if you did just arrive at the audition and didn't have much time to look over the script, you're giving us some important information about you when you tell us how unprepared you are. You're telling us that you need time with a script and aren't very good at quick study. Our scripts are rewritten every day on the set; every set operates this way. Many times the writers are right there on the set and we are improving the script as we shoot. We need to know that you can handle this typical type of workday. Keep in mind that on a set if we change dialogue, you'll have to unlearn dialogue that you had previously learned, and then relearn the new dialogue. That's even harder than just learning the original dialogue. So the last thing you want to tell us is that you are not a quick study.

If you're auditioning for a TV show, you should have watched the show and know the characters beforehand. Watch a few episodes of every show on the air at least a few times each year. You would read differently for one show as opposed to another; each show has its own flavor. You would even read differently depending on who you're playing opposite. For example, I doubt you would read a line the same opposite Danny DeVito as opposite Arnold Schwarzenegger.

I've had actors come in and ask, "Is this a comedy or a drama?" Actors will ask these types of questions about a show that has been on the air for many years! It doesn't make any sense to ask such questions and shows a lack of professionalism on the actor's part. A variation of the above comment that really upsets TV people is, "I haven't seen the show since I don't watch TV." This tells everyone that TV is beneath you. Hello! What are you saying, we're not high enough up the food chain for you?

Keep a card file on every person you meet in this business, to help you prepare for auditions. If you read for a particular casting director and/or director, your card file should record what you talked about, the name of the project, etc. The next time you meet that person you will have some reference to fall back on.

Before we move on to the next apology, let me reemphasize that being unprepared is everyone's top gripe about you. Please, don't ever show up to an audition without being prepared. Period!

The next apology will happen when you're about halfway through the script. You'll mess up in the middle of the reading because most actors mess up in readings. But you'll think you're unique; that you're the only person who has messed up that day. We don't care if you mess up. It doesn't affect our casting decisions.

As an actor, you feel the need to discuss the mess-up, which becomes a problem because you're now making the goof look much worse than it actually was. How do you do this? First, you'll start communicating your mistake to us visually. You'll wrinkle up your nose or mouth and stare at the script as though the writer messed up. Then the apology will become verbal. "Tom, I really messed up. Can I start over again?" The short answer is, "No." The unspoken answer is, "I've seen this script performed hundreds of times. Please don't start over!"

It's generally a bad idea to ask to start over once you are past a page or two, especially when reading for the director and/or producer. In your first meeting with the casting director, it is more acceptable. Either way, it's a judgment call. When you are auditioning for the casting director, you could possibly ask, "May I try another reading with a really different interpretation?" In other words, don't, and I repeat don't, ask to do it over again because you think you gave a poor reading. If this is the real reason you want to do it over again, fine, but don't let anyone know that.

Definitely don't ask to start over again just because you lost your place in the script. Take a moment, find your place and move on. Nobody cares that you paused for a few seconds to find where you were in the script. But keep in character as you search for your place. In real life, people often lose their place and have to think of what to say next. It will enhance your audition if you just think like the character would think in those circumstances and move on.

And, if you're given permission to do it another way, make sure you really read it another way. Otherwise, you're just emphasizing that you have no range or creativity. Use this technique sparingly. And frankly, if you do really have two different ways of doing it, you should give it your best shot the first time around.

When people start over again, they hardly ever perform it any better the second time. I can literally count on one hand the rare occasions where someone started over and actually did a better performance, much less changed any minds in the room. Usually when someone starts over, we're wondering why that actor wasted our time when it wasn't any better the second time around. If you are given a second chance, definitely don't ask for a third!

In effect, when you stop and ask to start over again, you're directing all of a sudden. Who do you think you are . . . . Spielberg, Hitchcock, Howard . . . . Logan? Okay, just joking on the last one. But please, let the director direct.

One reason actors want to start over is because they try to memorize the material and not have the script in their hands when doing the actual audition. Unless asked otherwise (and even if you have it memorized), I recommend holding the script in your hands during the audition. If your memory is so bad that you can hide your own Easter eggs, fine. The audition is not a memory contest.

When you have a script memorized, you're telling us, "This is as good as it's going to get." In other words, you're doing a *performance*. When you glance at the script, even if you did memorize it (which, again, I advise against), that's a *cold reading*. Psychologically, *cold readings* are going to get better, but *performances* are not. Many times an actor walks out of an audition and someone in the room turns to me and says, "Wow, what a great cold reading. I can't wait to see his performance." We're taking into account that you haven't memorized it yet and that it will be even better when you have had time to do so.

When you do memorize a script, you become kind of locked into the way you want to perform it. It makes it harder for us to direct you in the audition. Nothing upsets a director more than giving an actor direction and the actor not taking that direction! This is a top gripe for directors.

Another thing happens when you memorize something very quickly. You don't look at the camera, or at the person to whom you are speaking; rather you stare at the camera or the person. You are actually seeing the script photographed in your mind; your eyes are "looking" back into your brain and "seeing" that script imprinted on it. Then we'll see a little jerk in your eyes every few seconds. Know what that is? It's the jerking motion of your eyes ending on one line and dropping down and back to the beginning of the next line as you see the script in your mind. Believe it or not, I've been asked by many clients, "Why are these actors staring and why are their eyes jerking?" Suffice it to say: Don't memorize the script even if you get it in advance, *unless asked to do so.*

Having said the above, sitcom people sometimes have a different take; they want to see the character and the performance in the audition. On the set there will be no time for character development, so they want to see in the audition what they're going to get before the shoot.

More apologies are to come. Next, when you finish auditioning, I will hear something like, "Well, Tom, I can do it differently. If you didn't like my performance, work with me. You're the director, I'm the actor, and together I think we can make this a lot better."

Sticking with our painter example: I've painted your house and say, "You know, we can change all of this. You just tell me what you want, and I think together we can make this a whole lot better.... Can I start over?" All of a sudden, my work doesn't look so good!

As you walk out the door, leaving the audition, yet another apology will come. This one will be visual. You'll walk out trying to give us the impression that "normally I do much better than this." This is as if the painter told you that he did a much better job for Ms. Jones down the street and that he can really do a much better job than he did for you. I don't think you'd be too impressed. Would you really care about what a great job he did for Ms. Jones?

Always walk out the door as though it was the best performance you've ever given and you can't imagine a performance from anyone getting much better than yours. A good or bad performance is all a matter of perception. Why do actors feel the need to help shape that perception towards the negative? So many times I've witnessed a terrible performance by an actor in an audition, only to see him improve the perception that his performance was better because of his attitude as he walked out the door.

I love female ice skaters. I know nothing about the sport but I can usually tell who did a good job and who didn't. From the time they finish skating to the time they sit down for the scoring numbers to be called, I've seen skaters kick the ice in frustration and became convinced they had done a bad job. After all, they know the profession much better than I do. I've seen other skaters jump up and down during this time. Then I knew they had done a great job. Again, they're the experts; they should know.

As actors, you can convince us you did a much better job than you actually did if you'll just act like you did a great job! Once I was directing this national soft drink ad when this actor (who had probably been to the Tori Spelling School of Hard Knocks) did a pretty poor job. In fact, she did a really poor job. Although her performance lacked a few things—talent . . . . direction . . . . focus . . . . believability . . . a purpose—she was jumping up and down for joy as she walked out the door. She was so proud of herself.

She was the worst person we saw for that entire job, yet the client turned to me after she left the room and said, "Yeah, she's really good." She convinced him she did a great job, where if she had just walked out of the room even neutral about her performance, he wouldn't have liked what she had done. This happens over and over again.

The opposite is also true. I've seen actors that we thought were brilliant, but by the time they were out the door we really disliked their performances. Actors do have an impact on what we think about their work. Look around you and you'll see examples of this in every profession and in your personal life.

In one audition I was sitting next to a very well-known television producer. After the actors had finished their first reading this producer would say to them, "Let's do it again, but this time make it better." The actors' typical response was, "What did you like . . . . dislike . . . . ?" That was the correct response from the actors.

This producer would then say, "I don't know, just make it better."

After about five actors had auditioned, I couldn't take listening to this producer anymore. So I said, "I think I'll talk to the actors because I'm not sure you know whether they are good or bad."

He said, "Oh, I know if they did a good job or not. I just watch the actors walk out the door. If they walk out like they did a good job, then they probably did a good job. If they walk out like they did a bad job, then they probably did a bad job. See, Tom, actors understand the acting profession much better than we do and they will always tell you how good or bad they were. You should listen to them." And to some extent he's correct. We do "listen" to what you tell us.

One thing actors don't realize is that comments they make are heard by us. At the end of an actor's recorded performance, the camera operator in the audition room will say, "Cut." The actor will usually swear, roll his eyes, shake his head, etc., without realizing that the time from the word "cut" to the time the operator pushes the "stop" button, about three or so seconds have passed. Those quick comments at the end of a performance are seen and heard by us! This happens more than you know.

Let's be honest: When I watch dailies (footage shot on that particular day), do you think I criticize my directing skills in front of the suits? Remember, the suits know less about directing than I do, just as the suits auditioning you probably know less about acting than you do. I am usually telling the suits how great the scene is and how happy I am with it. Pardon the expression, but follow suit!

CHAPTER TWO
Don't Beg

Begging comes in many different forms, but basically most actors beg in an audition. It wouldn't be so bad if we were only seeing a few actors, but hearing actor after actor beg becomes very old, very fast. It is also embarrassing for everyone in the audition room.

We know you want the job. That's why you're at the audition. We are on your side; we're pulling for you; we want you to be great. After all, we have to keep auditioning until we find an actor for each part, so we want to like you. Think of auditioning as you would going to see a movie in the theatre, you want to enjoy the film. You don't want to feel as though you have wasted your time and money viewing a particular film, and we don't with your audition either.

Begging won't help you look professional in anyone's eyes. When you start begging, we almost don't want to like you anymore. And it's not just actors that beg. Crew members do the same thing. Everyone in this business wants to work; we're all in the same boat here.

Actors shouldn't forget that directors, producers and casting directors have to look for work also. No one's job is secure in this business. Actors tend to look at producers and directors and think they're always busy. Wrong! What happens when a producer's show is canceled? He's out looking for another show to produce. He'll have to go out and "audition" for another show by showing copies of other projects he has produced. And yes, future employers of mine look at the last project or two that I directed. Being in that same boat, we understand the begging. And don't think we haven't done some begging ourselves and will probably do some more begging in the future, which is probably the main reason why we don't like it when you do it.

Women, let's be blunt: When you're on a date, is begging an attractive trait? Perhaps at some age it will be, but in general it's not! Doesn't a man begging to go out on a date with you make him become much less attractive? On that date, if a guy begs a woman for "love" (work with me) he probably has much less chance of getting that love than if his attitude is, "We're just out to have a good time. No 'favors' expected here." I'm not saying a guy is going to get anywhere with you on a date, but wouldn't he have a better chance if his entire goal on that date wasn't just to obtain love from you? (Did I put that diplomatically?)

The same is true in an audition. You'll have a much better chance of getting a job if you don't beg for it. Stated emphatically, "Your chances are very slim if you do beg."

"The Speech"

Almost every actor gives us what we call, "The Speech." If you've been on an audition you've probably given some form of the speech. If I have lunch with five other directors and I say, "I heard the speech two hundred times today," all five will know exactly what I'm talking about.

The speech goes something like this: "You know, I was sitting in the lobby reading this script and I was thinking to myself, 'This character is me . . . . I have lived the life of this character . . . . This character was written for *moi*.' "

Number one: We don't care. Number two: We don't care. Number three: We don't care. Number four: Who cares? Number five: We don't believe you. Every actor that walks in the door tells us how right they are for this particular role.

If I am looking for someone for the part of a nurse, every actress that walks in the door will tell me she's a nurse. We're not looking for a nurse! We're looking for an actor . . . . That's why we're having auditions. If we were looking for a nurse, we'd go to a hospital!

Gimmicks Equal Begging

Using gimmicks is begging! I can't even begin to mention all of the weird things actors do to get into someone's office. I know you've seen actors on talk shows tell stories about the things they did to get a part, but you're only hearing the success stories. And to some extent, times have changed. In the old days everyone had more time for such things. So, unless you have something incredibly original (and even then I'd think twice), gimmicks are basically not a good way to go.

If one more actor sends me a dinner roll with a note tied to it stating, "I want a role," I'm going to tie him up and force him to listen to an entire Britney Spears' CD. If one more actor sends me a shoe with the attached note, "Just trying to get my foot in the door," I might tie him to the stereo and take him to a high crime area. These, and dozens more, are not original gimmicks. Usually, gimmicks are a bad way to try to get into someone's office.

Don't Lie to Us—That's Begging!

Lying is a form of begging. Directors sit in auditions for a living and we've become pretty adept at spotting truth from fiction. You're not going to get away with being dishonest with us, because there are so many ways for you to get caught. The main way directors catch you is by checking the Internet Movie Database (www.imdb.com), commonly known in the industry as the IMDB. Visit this website and see for yourself.

You'll be amazed at the information this website contains. It lists who directed a certain project, and who stars in it and their credits; and much more. I would suggest that in advance you obtain all the information you can about everyone you're going to see in a particular audition, by using this website. Many times you won't know the names of the producer(s) and director beforehand, but if you do know whom you're going to meet, it wouldn't hurt to do a little research on them.

The Beverly Theory

Begging in an audition indicates an actor's lack of self-confidence. You talk yourself into or out of confidence. Let me illustrate it this way: When I was in college way back when meat, potatoes, and gravy were considered a balanced meal, I always had to have proof of everything. I couldn't take anything for granted. During my senior year, I had to write a thesis for my final psychology project. I had already written about the mating habits of the female frog and other interesting subjects, so I had to search hard for something to top my previous efforts.

Finally, I decided to test an old idea that I had heard many times, but wasn't sure if it was true. I rounded up three of my college buddies, all of whom were ready for any kind of mischief.

At ten o'clock in the morning I had one of my buddies just happen to stroll by Beverly in the secretary's office of the psychology department. He struck up a conversation about the flu. Beverly and my friend conversed for a long time about how everyone was running out and receiving their flu shots. Beverly said that she had not received one of those shots and my friend advised her to do so as soon as possible. She responded that she felt fine, but would think about my friend's suggestion.

At twelve noon that same day, I sent another devil to Beverly's office. This particular guy told Beverly she looked pale and tired, and suggested that she start getting more sleep. Beverly acknowledged that she had been a little tired all day, but that she felt okay.

Two o'clock rolled around and another buddy of mine sauntered into the office and told Beverly that she looked as though she were coming down with that terrible flu that everyone on campus has. He even suggested a good doctor for Beverly to go see. Beverly responded that she hadn't been feeling well all day.

At four o'clock I (the worst devil of all) went into Beverly's office to pick up some papers for the next semester's registration. I mentioned to Beverly that she "should go home immediately" because she looked as though she could use the rest. I also mentioned that her face looked a little pale and that perhaps she should go to the campus hospital and have her temperature taken. I suggested that she do this at once so the rest of us wouldn't get infected.

Not only did Beverly leave at one minute after four that afternoon, but she didn't return for four days. Was Beverly really sick? Yes. But what was the cause?

Okay, I'm a devil. And, yes, that's a true story. The point I'm making is, if something is suggested to you or you tell yourself something long enough, you tend to accept it as reality. Psychologists call this the "self-fulfilling prophecy" theory. We'll call it the "Beverly Theory."

By now you're wondering what the Beverly Theory has to do with begging. Everything! The cause behind begging is the lack of confidence in your acting abilities. And it's your attitude that could be the most important factor in your success (or lack thereof) in Hollywood, California, or Hollywood, Florida. If you believe that the actors who are working professionally are better than you, and decide that you really don't have much chance to succeed in this business, then save yourself some time and give this book to a friend. Without a positive attitude about your future in this business, this book won't do you any good.

When you beg you have accepted the suggestion that you're not really good enough to compete; that you need to beg to give yourself the edge. Unfortunately, it accomplishes just the opposite.

Would I Hire a Beggar?

Put yourself in the shoes of a suit spending millions of dollars on the project that an actor comes in to read for. The actor is obviously insecure, apologetic, and a beggar; he's nervous. Perhaps he spent more time in the bathroom than did the Tidy Bowl man. And even for a small part you're resting thousands of dollars on him personally.

Would you take a chance with that actor or would you instead hire someone who came in to read with a certain air of confidence?

Ask yourself: "Would I hire myself, were I the money man?" Consider the competition. Would you spend big bucks on a name actor or an actor with a lot of credits, who you knew could do the job, or on a nervous someone like yourself? If you aren't confident that you can do the job and do it well, then don't expect directors to feel confident that you can.

You already have enough working against you by going into the acting profession. Everyone does, so don't add to it by begging, which only shows the director that you aren't the right person for the job. The director started sizing you up when you walked into the audition. By giving us the speech (begging), you are starting off by giving a terrible impression of your lack of confidence in your acting abilities.

Sob Stories

Don't give us the "sob story," either. We hear them more than you can imagine. "I would really love to have this job, not for me, but for my little brother Joey . . . . so that he can have the operation, and maybe he can learn to run, jump and play like all of the other little boys."

Or we hear that actors can't pay their rent. (We're not welfare workers. We have our own troubles. We don't need to hear about yours.) Yes, I can certainly sympathize with you. Directors have been there and many will be there again! I don't, however, know of any director who will put his career on the line just because an actor has not been successful at finding an acting job.

How about this story: "I don't really know what to do with this part because I'm not really right for this role"? Boy, talk about sabotaging your own audition! And I hear this more than you realize. I can't go to a producer and say, "You know, I have no creative ideas for this project and I think I'm not the right director for this film, but could you just give me the job anyway?"

I don't want to hear this one: "No one will come see the play I'm currently in." In an audition, an actor should never drop off flyers about his play to the director and/or producer. Do you see the begging element here? It will drive the casting director nuts and I doubt that casting director will bring you in for future roles.

The Dreadful Question

Rattling off your acting credit list to that very common and dreadful question someone will ask you in auditions, "Tell me about yourself" is .... you guessed it .... begging. I have never asked an actor this question, and I doubt I ever will, but many directors and casting directors do ask it. We have your resume in front of us and can read it for ourselves and not waste anyone's time.

In one day, after hearing a few hundred credit lists, we're confusing what actor went with what list; at some point they all start to sound alike. Imagine if twenty people walked up to you today and recited a shopping list. I bet at the end of the day you couldn't tell me much about the people who gave you the lists, what was on each list, and who went with what list! Multiply those twenty lists by another twenty, and that's the number I'll listen to each day, because every actor works their credit list into the conversation.

Take into account that I'm seeing people day after day for this part. You can see that the above amount is multiplied many more times before a role is cast. When that question is asked, we just want to hear you speak. Tell us something interesting that shows off your personality. Don't make your answers so introverted that you can't even lead in silent prayer. We want to see your personality. We want to get to know you a little better before the reading. Try to talk about something other than your acting credits.

On the other hand, if you're the oratorical equivalent of a blocked punt, don't go on and on to the point I'm visualizing the Duck tape over your mouth. Actors like this don't need an introduction .... they need a conclusion. Time is flying in an audition, and you're trying to hijack it. To keep babbling on and on about nothing is another sign of nervousness. When you babble you start to look so goofy that Disney might sue you for copyright infringement. Sometimes I'm not looking at a watch; I'm looking at a calendar! (More on interviewing will be discussed in Chapter Twelve.)

Don't Be Impolite

Being nice and polite, on the other hand, is not begging. Be nice to everyone because you might not know who's who. When I was an actor way back when kids were belted and tires weren't, I was starring in a film being shot for Paramount Studios. Five of the actors, including myself, had Winnebagos for dressing rooms since we were on location. One day it was pouring down rain, a rare thing in Los Angeles, and all of us, with the exception of one star, let the "extras" climb into our Winnebagos.

That one star didn't let anyone into his dressing room, so about ten extras had to stand out in a cold, hard-driving rain for about an hour. Guess what? One of those extras is now a suit at one of the top studios in town! Because of that incident, when this star comes into audition, this same suit just never "finds that actor right for the part." That was over 25 years ago and he still remembers!

So I never downplay the importance of being nice to everyone. And I mean everyone. Some of the most powerful people in this industry are secretaries. They let us know what's going on in the audition waiting room. Being polite doesn't mean, "kissing up." You know the difference. As Mason said to Dixon, "We have to draw the line somewhere." Show respect for everyone in the room.

We try to be nice to you so we would appreciate you returning the favor. I look at all actors who are auditioning as though they are going to be stars someday. Maybe I'll be begging them to work in one of my films in the future. (Hey, sometimes directors beg, too!)

I repeat: You should be nice to everyone. You never know what that person will be doing in the future. *Be careful of the toes you step on today; they may be connected to the ass you'll be kissing tomorrow.*

"Crashing" an Audition

"Crashing" an audition is begging! You know what I mean—some actors find out about an audition and then just show up. I very strongly recommend that you don't do this. You have no idea what we're looking for. Maybe you think you're perfect for this audition because everyone in the lobby is your exact physical type. But you might not know that we're looking for someone who can skydive! When you walk into the audition room and we ask you about your skydiving experiences and you say, "Huh?," you've shed a bad light on the casting director who, it appears, didn't do his job. You think this sets kindly with the casting director and with us? Please rethink crashing auditions.

"Begging" comes in many different forms. Whether you give us the speech, perform gimmicks, lie, engage in sob stories, rattle off your credit list, or crash an audition, you're making a fatal mistake of which, unfortunately, most of your competition is guilty.

CHAPTER THREE

Don't Hang Around the Audition So We Can Tell You How Good or Bad You Were

Frankly, when you're hanging around in the audition room waiting for us to give you some clue as to how you did, we're actually not sure. And even if we were, we'd change our minds so many times that our original impression will become moot. Your performance will stand out as good or as bad depending on who comes in before you and who comes in after you. Casting is a comparison game. Whatever you may believe, there's no real standard on what is considered a good or a bad performance in an audition until everyone has been seen.

Fifty people might have come in before you who are brilliant, making you look dreadful. On the other hand, fifty people might come in after you who are awful, and you will look great. It all depends on how you fit into the mix. So basically any standard on what would be considered a good or a bad performance is constantly evolving as we audition more and more actors.

I can compare the changing standard to the movement of stocks in the market. Let's say you are heavily invested in the market and you woke up this morning and found that the Dow Jones Industrial Average was down five hundred points. At the end of the day it had risen and was down only one hundred points. You would be thrilled for that one hundred-point loss.

Then again, let's say that when you woke up this morning the Dow was ahead by five hundred points, but at the day's end it was down one hundred points. You'd be incredibly depressed over that hundred-point loss. It's the exact same one hundred-point loss, but what happened before and what happened after determines how you feel about it. The one hundred points is neither good nor bad. It all depends on what happens before the loss and after the loss. To some extent, our feelings about your audition follow the same logic. Most directors won't admit this, but in reality, what precedes and what follows is what shapes our beliefs about your performance.

By the time you arrive home from an audition, we will have changed our minds about your performance depending directly on how many actors we've seen, from the time you left the audition to the time you arrived home. Each auditioning actor reshapes our opinions of the people who went before or after him.

Think of it another way: Have you ever dated someone for a long, long, long time—three, four weeks? You finally arrived at the point that you couldn't stand the way he eats, smells, drives, etc., so you go out with twenty other people. All of a sudden that first person doesn't look so bad anymore. Think of how many times you have changed your mind on whether someone was a good or bad mate for you, depending on who you have been out with since. With each new person that you date, don't you find yourself reevaluating all the people you dated before? All of a sudden some former mates look much worse, and some look much better. Casting is no different.

Think back to that one person whom you dated years ago and who you're no longer with. At the time, you thought that person was God's gift to your gender. You thought that if you didn't marry this person life as you knew it would be over for you. Everyone has that one person. Now you look back on that relationship and are wondering, "Exactly what type of heavy medication was I on at the time that made me like that person?"

The same thing happens with auditions. We've had people come into auditions at nine in the morning who made us think we had died and gone to heaven because they were Playboy material and terrific actors. But by four in the afternoon we couldn't remember who they were or why we liked them.

Conversely, I've had people come in at ten in the morning that we thought were absolutely horrible. But by five in the afternoon we had signed them to a two-picture deal. There is no logic to the casting process, so quit wasting your time looking for it.

As the day goes on we become either more picky or less picky. In other words, someone that wouldn't have been called back had she auditioned in the morning might be called back if she had come in the afternoon. Someone that didn't appeal to us in the morning might become more appealing in the afternoon because we weren't thrilled with what we saw in the morning. The opposite, of course, is also true.

Maybe by the afternoon we're finding that we're calling back too many people. Or maybe we're finding out that we're not calling back enough actors. So the standard, if there ever really was one, has changed as to what is considered callback material.

Look at it this way: Suppose you're a male and you really need a date this evening. It's been awhile, okay? (You know who you are!) So you head on down to the local pub. For argument's sake, suspend your disbelief and let's suppose there's no alcohol involved. (Work with me, guys.) Remember, you really *need* a date this evening. About eight-thirty you spot a woman who doesn't seem attractive to you. How does she look at midnight?

We won't discriminate: If we reverse the sex roles it works the same. The principle hasn't changed. Your feelings toward someone do change as time passes and/or you meet other people. Your standards in the bar situation did change over the course of a few hours. So do ours in auditions.

This is why you shouldn't put *any* stock in anything we say to you at that moment. It means absolutely nothing. We may truly believe what we're saying at that moment, but so do half the people who say, "I do" on their wedding day, and then "don't." Some actors get excited because we ask them if they are available. This means nothing.

We ask just about everyone this question; it's standard. But then you shouldn't get your underwear in a tizzy if we don't ask. That means absolutely nothing, either.

During your reading, don't keep glancing at us to see our reactions. Actors want to know how they're doing during the actual reading, but our reactions at the time mean nothing. Keep in mind that we really don't know at that point. Our assessment of you will get better or worse, depending on who comes in after you.

Many directors are poker-faced anyway. They try not to give too much encouragement or too little. Most directors are pretty decent people! By glancing at us during your actual reading, we kind of feel obligated to laugh in the right places and show sadness in the right places. This gets very tiring when seeing hundreds of actors in the same day. It also takes our concentration away from your performance. It may sound strange to say, but it is uncomfortable for us. You're trying to force us to let you know how good or bad we thought you were in that audition, and we can't at that point.

If a director cuts you off in an audition and tells you that he's seen all he needs to see, don't necessarily take this negatively. I think saying this borders on rude behavior and I don't do it, but some directors do. True, it could be a bad sign. Maybe you are just so wrong for this character that he doesn't want to waste any more of his or your time. Or perhaps you are so right for this part that he doesn't want to waste anyone's time because, at least at this point, he thinks he's going to call you back. Again, you mustn't judge anything by this behavior either.

Some actors become paranoid if someone in the room doesn't say much to them after the reading. Maybe we are so blown away by your audition that we're stunned. Or maybe you were so awful that we just have nothing to say. Or maybe we're not sure yet whether we liked your performance or not and aren't ready to make any comments. Again, you can judge nothing about the audition from how much or how little someone talks to you after your actual reading.

Time Spent in the Audition Means Nothing

While we're on the subject, don't try to guess how your perform-ance went over based on the amount of time you spent in the actual audition room. Actors will sometimes think to themselves, "Well, per-haps I have a great shot at it because they kept me in the room for about ten minutes and everyone else was in there for about five."

There's some rationale to this. If we weren't interested, why would we waste time with you? But then again, perhaps you are physically perfect for this part, but your performance was so lacking that we're going to keep you here as long as possible to see if we can get some kind of performance out of you.

At other times actors will think, "They're probably not interested in me because I was in there for only five minutes and everyone else was in there for ten." There's rationale for this kind of thinking, too. Perhaps you were totally wrong for this role so we want you out of the room as soon as possible. But, possibly you're so right for this part and your reading was so terrific that we don't want to give you time to reverse our thinking. We're getting you out the door to start moving the audition process along a little faster, because, at least at that point, we believe we're going to call you back.

Directors Bargain Roles

One reason you can't "read" us is because many times we "bar-gain" roles. I hate to talk about this, but this is an honest book, so let's be blunt. You won't hear many people talk about this because, in the scheme of things, very few people actually have the opportunity to sit in on auditions. But I think it's an important aspect of the audition process. "Bargaining" roles happens much more in feature film casting than in television casting, usually because there are many more roles in a feature film to be cast with many more variables than for a tele-vision show. But it happens in every medium.

Let's suppose that on Monday actor "A" comes into an audition. The suits are thrilled with this actor. The director also wants this actor for the part. The suits talk about how much they like actor "A" and the director realizes that he has a bargaining chip. So despite his preference, the director might say, "Well, maybe he'll do, but let's keep looking. He didn't 'rock me' as much as he did you guys."

Now, on Wednesday actor "B" comes in the door to read for a totally different role. The director is crazy about this actor, but the suits aren't "sold" on him, so the director puts his bargaining chip forward. He'll say, "Well, okay, I'll tell you what I'm going to do. I'll give you actor 'A' if you'll give me actor 'B.'"

This is a win-win situation for the director and actors. Both the actors were cast, so they're happy. The director got the actor he wanted, so he's happy. Sometimes I've walked on sets and there's hardly an actor who was my first choice because I had to do so much bargaining, yet I ended up with a cast with which I'm extremely happy. I'm happy with my entire cast. After all, I bargained to get them, but that doesn't necessarily mean they were all my first choices.

The above might explain why the director didn't act as excited about you after your audition as you would have wanted him to. You might feel your audience in an audition couldn't have been colder if you had performed in a morgue. Was the director "playing the game" and acting cool in front of the powers that be, although he's actually crazy about you? If he was, that way he can settle for you later, even though he might have wanted you all along. I don't like this game, but we all seem to get caught up in it.

Leaving the Audition Room

As you slowly walk towards the door, don't give false compliments to the director. Being nice is one thing, but being phony is another. I've had actors tell me how much they enjoyed a film I directed, even before it had been completely edited! Ten states could be using one of my films as capital punishment and I'd still receive compliments. This is another reason you should do research on the people you're going to meet in an audition. It's okay to compliment a director, if you really did see one of his films and enjoyed it. Just keep your compliments genuine.

As you're leaving, or entering for that matter, you don't need to shake all of our hands. I wouldn't shake hands with anyone unless they extend their hand first. Think how many actors we're seeing in a day. Actors who come in coughing and sneezing and want to shake our hands make us uncomfortable. Some directors I know like a wide desk or table in front of them that makes it difficult for an actor to shake their hand.

If we offer our hands, however, or if you strongly feel it is appropriate to shake someone's hand, then do so, making it firm and looking him in the eyes. Don't make it wimpy or so fast that we aren't sure it was a shake. On the other hand, don't shake hands forever. I don't want to feel attached to someone.

I make it a habit when I'm speaking at a large university for an extended period to give everyone a restroom break. My pet peeve is walking into the restroom and having an actor, who has just finished at the urinal, zip up and then walk over to shake my hand. Yuck! Although this example is much more extreme than at an audition, the principal is the same. I know directors who keep liquid soap under the table and use it after each actor shakes their hand. With eight or so people in the room, it is time-consuming to shake everyone's hand, especially when dozens of actors are waiting in the lobby to be auditioned. It's a judgment call on your part. Bottom line: Err on the side of not shaking.

Although I love hugs, and we all need a little hug once in a while, we don't need a hug at the end of your audition. Even if an actor knows me very well, a hug is inappropriate. It makes you look cheesy, and it is very uncomfortable for me. It takes away my power in decision-making because the others in the room begin to think I want this person because she's a friend. Similarly, for you to hug the casting director in the lobby puts her in an awkward position with the other actors waiting to audition.

Kids are the worst about this "hugging thing," because Mommy told them to do it. I love kids more than the next guy and have two of the greatest kids that have ever lived. On a set, when I've been working for weeks with a particular child and he does a fabulous take, fine, come hug me. But in today's social environment, we don't like to hug kids we don't know, especially in an audition. It's totally inappropriate.

I've encouraged you not to hang around too long, but this isn't to say you should run out the door either. Some actors can't wait to get out the door even as they are still performing. I realize you sometimes want to get out because you're so unhappy with your performance, but you're going to act like you did a great job, so don't be off quicker than a prom dress.

Why do actors want to hang around? Some want to see which pile we put their photos on. You could make the argument that if your photo goes into the smaller pile that would be a plus, but it wouldn't necessarily be a smart bet. I've already said that you're wasting your time trying to figure out what we thought of your audition. Photos will be switched from one pile to another frequently during the course of the day. Where yours is put when you leave may have no bearing on where it will end up. Secondly, don't assume the smaller pile is better, because it could be the "definitely not" pile.

Other actors try to read our notes. Because this is so common, some people jot down comments in a personal code. I can't say it enough times: Our ideas about you will change throughout the course of the audition process as we see other actors. Even if you could read our notes, our comments are not written in stone. Don't try to look over our shoulders.

Despite what I've said, let me add something: Yes, you should get out of the actual audition room fairly quickly and without lots of chat, unless we encourage it. But once you're out of the main room, don't run out the lobby door too fast. Take your time signing out and then leisurely leave. The reason for this is, if you just met the director and/or producer, they may talk about you for a few minutes after you leave, and for a variety of reasons may decide that they want you to read with someone else. We didn't know that at the time you were walking out of the audition room; we hadn't discussed it with each other until after you left. If you're still in the lobby, we can call you back in easily. Whether we ask you to come back or not, again, don't take it to mean much more than there must be some interest. Or perhaps that we didn't have anyone else in the lobby to read your part with the next person auditioning.

When you get home from the audition, you'll probably phone your agent for a report. Every agent will tell you that when an actor phones and says she thinks she got the part, that she did a great job, the odds are that the actor won't be called back. When an actor phones and says he totally messed up the audition and thinks he won't be called back, he probably will be. It's strange, but it happens this way most of the time.

Bottom line: Quit trying to figure out auditions and the rationale that goes along with them. You are wasting your time.

CHAPTER FOUR

Don't Ask Us What We're Looking For

Number one: We don't know. Number two: We don't know. Number three: We don't know. Number four: Who knows? And even if we did know, after each actor left the audition we would change our minds. Our train of thought doesn't always have a caboose. And besides, no one in the room agrees with what we're looking for. We're all meandering to a different drummer. When lunchtime rolls around I won't even be able to get everyone in the room to agree on the pizza toppings.

Although by the time the audition is over I would've heard these lines being delivered hundreds of times, you might be at the beginning of the audition process. If this were the case, I would be hearing them for the first time. Maybe we haven't yet formed an opinion how we want the lines delivered. Even if we have, we change our minds constantly.

This is one of many reasons why you should bring in a few different headshots to an audition. For a commercial audition, bring your theatrical headshot, too. Conversely, for a theatrical audition, bring your commercial headshot as well. (The differences between theatrical and commercial headshots are explained in Chapter Nine). This allows us to pick one over the other depending on what we "think" we're looking for at that moment. Bring in multiple copies of the same headshot, so more than one person in the room can have one. Never assume that because your agent sent us your photo and resume, or because you've already been there once, we don't need another headshot. Be prepared. I don't want to hear, "My headshot is in the car. Do you want me to go get it?" Hello!

Asking the director what he's looking for is basically asking him how to do your job. Show us what we're looking for, because we really don't know. Haven't I mentioned that no one in the audition room agrees with what we're looking for?

Your question would be like me masquerading as a plumber and coming to your house for an interview drumming up business to "plumb" for you. I show up and ask, "Now, how do you want these pipes connected? I can use plastic, or steel, or whatever. What do you think?" By this point you're thinking you want another plumber.

Asking us what we're looking for, when the director probably hasn't even really decided yet because it might be early in the game, puts me in the position of having to make commitments about the character in front of the suits and/or ad agency account executives. Maybe I'm not ready to commit to it yet.

Nor does a director want to give very much information to each actor, because some actors will come in and give him something much more interesting than he originally had in mind. In fact, some actors definitely will. Then the director can take credit for it!

Other Questions You Shouldn't Ask

Don't ask us for rehearsal time in the audition room. If you arrived at the audition early, you've already had time to do that. Sometimes actors ask to rehearse first so that we can give them direction with regards to the part. We don't have time to do this with every actor that we audition. We're seeing two hundred performances that day; this would make it four hundred. That request is another way of asking us what we are looking for.

This isn't the time to ask us how much the job pays. This is so presumptuous on the actor's part. We probably aren't sure ourselves at that point. Nothing has been negotiated. Amounts might depend on whether we get a name actor or a newcomer. Secondly, aren't you supposing that we're interested in you? This may or may not be the case. I know that there are acting teachers who advise their students to ask this question because they think it starts the actor believing they already having the job. Nonsense!

You should know that most actors work for "scale plus ten"; that means union scale, and an extra 10 percent is thrown in for the agent. In fact, recently the pay for many speaking roles has slightly decreased. The reason is because stars are making such high salaries these days that we have to save money for them. We are scraping money from other actors to pay for the star(s). Sound unfair? Remember, this is not a fair business! Some day it will be unfair in your favor!

Don't ask us when we are having callbacks. First, we probably aren't sure ourselves. Secondly, the odds of you being called back aren't very high, so we consider this a waste of time to talk about. Sometimes an actor will ask, "When should I expect to hear from you?" How can we possibly answer that question? Usually the answer would be, "Never." But, of course, we don't want to say that. And even if we do plan to call you back at that moment, we could change our minds as the day progresses.

Don't ask us how many days' work your character will receive. To begin with, it's not "your character," and again, we probably don't know. Nor should you ask us what date(s) "your character" will be working. If it's a feature film, we probably won't know until the day before that character is to begin work. Whether we know or not, our minds are not on the shooting schedule at this point. Our minds are focused on finding the right actors for the parts we're casting.

We may not even know yet who is starring in the project, so don't ask. If we do know, it's nothing we want to discuss, because negotiations with that star might possibly still be taking place. If we haven't made this information available to your agent or the trade papers, there's a reason.

Don't ask us what acting method you should use in the audition. Most people in the room don't understand all the acting methods out there. We don't care what method you use or even if you use any method at all, as long as you are believable and give us a performance that can be edited. This goes along with asking us what your motivations should be. You're trying to get us into a lengthy discussion about the character and time does not permit this. Some actors do this to try and show us their knowledge of acting. Show us that in your reading!

We don't want to be asked for acting advice and tips. We don't want to discuss actors' careers on our time and at our expense. We don't have any tips for you in an audition. An audition is not a career consulting session.

Don't ask us to wait while you fumble around in your briefcase or folder looking for your headshot and resume. Have them out and ready to hand to whomever asks for it in the audition room. Waiting for people to get their act together is a waste of our time.

It's generally a bad idea to ask to perform extra material. In film and TV auditions, some actors will ask if they can perform their monologues. TV and film directors are usually not interested in monologues, because it tells us nothing about how you will "play and react off of" another actor. (This will be covered more fully in Chapter Eleven.) TV and film are visual mediums. Monologues are much more common in stage auditions, where they aren't considered "extra" material.

When you perform more material, you generally look less favorable. It's like going on a trip with a potential mate you've spent very little time with and that you think is wonderful. Afterwards you decide this person isn't so wonderful after all. Or if your high-school friend becomes your college roommate, that roommate may be much less appealing to you after spending more time together.

If the director does give you some direction, don't ask if you can go out to the lobby and work on it for awhile. This really scares directors. What happens when we get on a set and each time the director gives you comments you want to think about it for awhile?

Take the new direction he gives you, apply it, and move on. This is not theatre acting where you have a lot of time to ponder direction. If an actor can't adapt on the set very quickly to direction, then the director is in serious trouble on that shoot.

An exception to the preceding would be if a screen director asked you to read for a totally different character than you originally read for, or if he asked you to read for the same character, but from different pages of the script than those he had you prepare. Then it would be perfectly acceptable, and advisable, to ask permission to leave the room for a few minutes to prepare.

If, however, you are auditioning for a play, then asking for a few minutes to work on new directions is acceptable. Stage actors have much more time to work on their characters than do their counterparts in television and film. The rehearsal time is much, much longer.

At the end of the audition, don't ask us if we liked your reading. Refer back to the entire last chapter!

The time to ask the most questions is before you audition for the director and/or producer. Ask questions, although only good ones, during your first meeting with the casting director. Don't ask him how to play a part. Certainly he'll help you in any way that he can since he's your friend in an audition. The casting director wants you to have as much information about the character as possible.

Bottom line: Once you're in the actual audition room with the director and/or producer, ask as few questions as possible.

Questions You Should Ask

You can ask, "Is there something about this character I should know?" After all, you might only be reading two pages of a hundred-and-twenty-page script. Or, "Is there something about this script I should know?" These are legitimate questions because you are obviously not given much information about the character for which you are reading. But, as I said, it is much better to ask questions during your initial meeting with the casting director than when you're meeting with the director and/or producer. It's okay to ask for clarification on something no matter whom is present.

Neither of these two questions are "how to act" or "how to play a part" questions. They are simply research questions that make the director think you want to have as much information as possible about the character. This would be the same as I, the plumber, asking you, "When you turn on the water, do you get sufficient pressure? Do you get hot and cold water?" I'm asking research questions, not asking you how to do my job.

After asking the above questions, you should ask, "How are you framing this?" Or, "Where are the frame lines?" This, of course, assumes your audition is being recorded. Once you get an answer, stay in those frame lines!

Asking about the frame lines signals to the director that you understand the limitations of the camera better than most actors do. Most directors will hold their hand flat and horizontal somewhere between their waist and neck area. This would signify the bottom part of the frame. That's all you'll get so you have to figure out the side and top frame lines.

To help you, think of television as a perfect square. In reality it's not, but it's close enough for our purposes. So if you use the bottom line as the bottom part of the square, you can fill in the sides and top. (Most auditions that are recorded are played back on the regular television format, not letter-boxed, hence the "almost" square formula.)

As well as signaling to the director that you understand basic framing, this lets you know how much room you have, or don't have, for head movement. In a screen audition you have practically none, but it's nice to know if you have enough headroom to turn your head from side to side without going out of frame. Don't rock from side to side. It drives directors crazy! Rocking makes it appear as though the actor has recently been on a boat in the ocean, lives on a fault line, or was in Dad's liquor cabinet the night before.

I once directed an Academy Award-winning actor who could hardly stand still. I was so frustrated that, one day when the actor was in his dressing room, I had his shoes nailed to the set floor. When he arrived on the set he had to put his feet in those shoes. You guessed it—I didn't have any problems with him rocking from side to side for the rest of the shoot!

It is also acceptable to ask us where you should focus your eyes, if it isn't obvious. In other words, does the person running the casting want you to look directly into the camera (common in single person, commercial auditions), at the "reader" in the room, at a dot on the wall, or somewhere else? In most TV and film auditions your focus will be on the other actor or the casting director, depending on who is reading the scene with you. But everyone has his quirks in this department, so it is perfectly acceptable to ask.

Obtaining Information About the Character

Check first with your agent to obtain a copy of the script and all the information you can about the character. Usually, your agent has that material and information. If your agent doesn't, then, as previously mentioned, you can check with the casting director's office to see if you can obtain a copy of the material to be read at the audition.

If either of those is not successful, then another way to get an idea about the character and obtain part of the script in advance is to log on to Showfax (www.showfax.com) and/or Castnet (www.castnet.com). Many of the film, TV, and commercial scripts are available from these outfits. They do charge fees, but the fees are definitely worth it if your agent doesn't get the sides to you or if they are not available to him.

Be aware that most directors don't cast by interpretation. In other words, even if your interpretation of the scene is way off base as we see it, it may have nothing to do with whether you're cast or

not. If a director casts you simply because you gave the same interpretation he has, he simply doesn't have much creativity and has
very little insight.

I can change interpretation very quickly and easily: "Be a little
meaner," and so on. What we're really looking for is whether we
believe the scene even with your strange interpretation. The fact
that you sound like an actor and not a real person is too difficult for
me to change on a set. But interpretation is easy to change, so quit
worrying about whether you're giving the same interpretation as
we have. Remember, we don't even agree on the interpretation
amongst ourselves. The more information you have about the character, the better off you will be in the long run in the interpretation
department.

I've said it is perfectly fine to ask for any clarification of something you don't understand and I strongly suggest that you do. Again,
this is research and is different than asking us how to play a part. Re-
strain yourself from asking us what we're looking for; the tendency is
there for you to query us about this. It must be—every actor asks!

CHAPTER FIVE

Don't Put Down Another Actor in the Audition

This is a huge no-no. You don't know who is "dating" whom in that room. I'm not joking here. Many actors have ruined their chances of getting a particular part because they mouthed-off about the person with whom they were reading after the other actor left the room first. Many times people in the room have relatives auditioning and many have no experience whatsoever.

"Unfair," you respond? Keep this in mind: Show business is unfair—always has been, always will be. Every business is unfair. People are promoted constantly in all fields simply because they know someone or are related to someone. Let's be honest here: I have two incredible sons and you can be assured that if I were holding an audition, my two sons would have an advantage!

Show business is no different than any other business. Show me someone who tells you that favorites aren't played, and I'll show you someone who has never sat in an actual audition.

This rule of not saying anything negative about your partner also applies for *anyone* sitting in an audition. I was directing a commercial for a national company when the client showed up an hour late. We start getting antsy when we get an hour behind in auditions, because union rules require the client to start paying the actors for any time we keep them in a commercial audition for over an hour.

When the client arrived I didn't even have time to introduce myself since the first actor came in right behind him. The actor read, and it was probably the worst audition I had ever seen. Believe me, I don't care how much of a newcomer you are, you would have shined in this audition if you had been reading for the same part. When the woman left, I crinkled up my nose and kind of said in a very high-pitched, sarcastic voice, "Who was that?"

"That's my daughter," the client said proudly. With my nose still crinkled and my voice still quirky and high-pitched, I responded quickly and to the point, "Oh, she's just marvvvvvvvvelous." He didn't know that I talked any differently since this was the first time we had ever spoken to each other. So I had to keep talking with my nose crinkled up and my high-pitched, quirky voice for two straight days of auditioning!

Unfortunately, some of my friends were coming in to audition. They had no idea why I was talking in a high-pitched, quirky voice with my nose all scrunched up. I'm sure I blew their concentration. I feel badly about that, but I wasn't about to lose a client over my stupidity.

The next day we were shooting the commercial and all was going great. I had a huge crew that was working like a perfectly oiled machine. Then all of a sudden, after eight hours of shooting, I noticed out of the corner of my eye that the client's car was arriving. I immediately yelled to the crew, "We're breaking for fifteen minutes."

The client exited his car and I went over to talk to him privately because I had to continue the nose and voice routine of the, "Who was that?" question in the audition. I mentioned to him that he didn't need to stay because everything was under control. In other words, I was trying to get him to leave so I wouldn't have to continue the weird routine in front of a huge crew.

He said, "Oh, no, I love to watch this stuff. I'm staying for the rest of the shoot."

I had to weigh what I should do. Which was more important to me—my humility or my paycheck, much less my career? You guessed it—my paycheck/career. With the weird voice and scrunched up nose, I immediately yelled out, "We're back, everyone." You could hear a pin drop. The crew was stunned. I had to continue the routine for the next four hours. It was obvious that everyone thought I had too many pigeons on my antenna. I learned a major lesson over those days: Don't put anyone down in an audition! And to answer your question, no, his daughter didn't get the part.

In another instance, I was called into a meeting regarding the possibility of directing a brand-new TV series. The pilot had already been shot and the backers were extremely unhappy with the way it had turned out. The producers showed me the pilot and afterwards wanted my comments.

As usual with being a director, I found myself in an extremely uncomfortable position. I was sitting with the creators, producers, writers, and a major well-known actor who was the star of the show (and also one of the producers) and they wanted me to tell them what was wrong with their work. (We'll refer to the star as Kitty Litter, although her name has been changed to protect the guilty.) The problem was, if I had told them everything that was really wrong with the show, I would have offended many egos and would have been thought of as being "difficult"—a nice term in show business referring to a jerk.

On the other side of the coin, if I had told them it was terrific, they wouldn't have wanted to hire me because I wouldn't have given them any incentive. They needed to know what I would do to make it better. So, being the up-front person that I am, I overly stated my objections to the way their show had been cast.

I started off with something to the effect of, "The lead girl is atrocious. She's an embarrassment to the show." In an attempt at humor, which apparently wasn't, I blurted out, "In fact, her parents should be shot for child abuse for enabling her to humiliate herself in front of millions of people." It was obvious to me that her parents hadn't won at genetic roulette. My opinions became even more blatant, but let's just leave it at that.

By the time I left the meeting, I realized that I had overstated my case and drove home thinking that I would probably never hear from these people again. In order to try to be nice, let me just say that the lead girl really wasn't right for the part.

Two months later I ran into a friend of mine who is a director of photography. He mentioned that he was the cinematographer on a particular TV show, which by coincidence was the same TV show whose lead actor I had massacred.

He devastated me by saying, "You know who plays the lead girl in the show?"

I said, "No, who?" I really didn't want to hear the answer.

He said, "That's Kitty Litter's daughter."

I realized I had been sitting next to the star of the show in that meeting and that I had been destroying her daughter's acting and personality. Wow, I really learned my lesson for the second time—never, ever, put anyone down in an audition.

Three weeks later the show's executive producer phoned. I said, "Susan, don't even bother to let me know what you thought about our meeting. Let's just hang up."

She said, "Not only do we want you to direct the next episode, but we'd like for you to direct the entire season."

There was an extremely long pause where no one spoke. Then she asked, "Tom, are you there?"

I questioned very slowly, "Was Kitty present during this discussion?"

"Oh, yes, she seemed to agree."

I couldn't believe what an incredible person Kitty must be. I had been destroying her daughter's performance in front of a dozen people and she was so above it all that she let that slide and did what she thought was best for the show.

During the two months of prep on the show, I worked on a preplanned speech that I was going to say to Kitty when I saw her again on the first day of shooting. It started out something like this, "Well, Kitty, you'll get to know my sense of humor and realize I was only kidding about your daughter . . . . ."

The more I rehearsed the speech, the phonier it became. So I decided that I was just going to come clean, take her aside the first day of shooting, and apologize with all my heart and all my might. The prep period was very uncomfortable for me, realizing I was going to have to face this woman and clear the air, since we were going to be working together for some time.

The first day arrived and I took Kitty into her dressing room and said, "Kitty, I'm extremely sorry for the horrific things I said about your daughter."

She asked, "What, exactly, did you say about my daughter?"

She was going to make me repeat all the things I had said. So, I stated, "Well, that you should be shot for child abuse for letting your daughter humiliate herself in front of millions of people and that she should be kept in a kennel during filming...." I went on and on and repeated everything I had said in that meeting.

She seemed stunned, and with good reason. It turned out that her daughter had taken over episode number two, but I had been shown the first episode and the girl in that one had been fired. I didn't know they had shot two episodes. I was hired because I was the only director who was honest about the original actor's performance.

Although this incident turned out in my favor, it is very safe to say that putting someone down in an audition is one of the worst things you can do. I certainly have learned my lesson and hope that this lesson will be beneficial to you.

What to Do With an Inexperienced Partner

Don't direct another actor in an audition. You can suggest some points to another actor, but be careful. Make sure you make it appear as though you're just giving the other actor a suggestion because it will help *you*. You should work out the scene together, but be careful how you handle this one.

As mentioned, you should never put down another actor in an audition. What do you do if that person really ruins your performance? Yes, another actor can make you look worse. If you're watching a play and ten actors are great and one is awful, the awful one pulls down the rest of the cast. Can't the director see through that? Maybe, and maybe not.

Realize first that even if you could read again with someone else that person might be just as bad, or even worse! You think not? Believe me, no matter how bad you think you or your scene partner were, there's always someone who was worse! You probably know this from dating!

If the person is really bad and you think you have nothing to lose, then there is one thing you can do, but do it sparingly. When the reading is over, start walking towards the door and let the other actor exit first. Then, when that actor is out of earshot, ask to read it with someone else; no put-downs in any way whatsoever. . . . just a straightforward question. This is only a last resort, especially when the director and/or producer are present. It is rare, but it has happened that the casting director will voluntarily try to save you by offering you another chance with another actor. The people in the room may or may not let you do it again, but whichever it is, don't take either side to be positive or negative.

Let's suppose we don't let you read it with someone else. One reason could be that we think you're so right for this part that we don't need you to do it again; we're already thinking about calling you back, so why waste everyone's time? Or it could be that you're just so wrong for this role that we don't want to bother. Or maybe we're just too far behind. If you see there are many people waiting in the lobby to read, it's probably best not to ask.

"Dissing" Your Agent

Although this chapter is about bad-mouthing another actor, let's take it a step further. As mentioned, don't bad-mouth anyone in an audition, and that goes for your agent, too. Those of us hearing auditions know most of the agents because we work with them on a daily basis. Most interactions with agents are by casting directors, but directors also know many of the agents in town. I can't tell you how many actors come into an audition and talk about all the work they're getting for themselves without the help of their "useless agent." You know what? We know this might be true; directors have agents, too.

But when you bad-mouth your agent in any way, we wonder immediately if your agent is the problem or if you're the problem. Sometimes it's the actor who is the problem. Is your attitude telling us that you're not doing enough work on your own? Maybe you're not hustling enough. If you've had a string of bad luck with agents, does that mean that you don't work well with people in general? It could be a red flag to a director who might have to work with you for a few months, or even years in the case of a TV series.

The people working in the entertainment community in Los Angeles and New York make up a small community. In fact, I might be "doing lunch" with your agent that day.

"Dissing" the Script

Not only should you refrain from putting any person down in the audition, don't put down the script either. I've had actors ask in auditions, "Who wrote this %&#$?" I sometimes have to answer, "I wrote this %&#$!" Even if I didn't write the script, the producer is there and he's paying for the %&#$. He doesn't want to hear about how bad the %&#$ is that he paid for. Guess what? The director probably thinks the script is %&#$, also. I've sat in auditions where we all thought the script was a disaster, but for an actor to come in and say so is wholly inappropriate. If you hate it, and chances are that you might, keep it to yourself.

Now you're thinking, "Well, if the director doesn't like the script, why is he directing it?" Directors are no different than actors when it comes to work. That's like asking an actor why he accepted a role if the script didn't work for him. The reason is the same for all of us.... We all need the work. Never forget that. There are very few people in this industry, and I mean very, very, very few who can pick and choose what projects they want to be involved with—very few!

Copping an Attitude

While we're on attitude, be careful that you don't have a bad one. Many actors come into an audition with a worse disposition than an untipped waiter. Such an attitude makes us wonder if the chip is on your shoulder, or in your head.

Some actors think it is "in-style" to be edgy. No, it's just rude. A director is going to have to spend a lot of time with you if you are cast. We like to work with people we like. Period! I have to judge how well you're going to get along with the rest of the cast and crew because we might be working together for an extended period of time.

Some actors act as though they don't want to be in our audition, but instead would rather be someplace else. This might be the case. Perhaps you would just as soon attend a funeral than an audition. However, this is your chosen profession, so act like you want to be in that audition. The director might not want to be there either. We have a hundred million other things to deal with than just casting.

Don't cop an attitude if the director whispers to someone during your audition, which happens frequently. A good many actors assume this is bad news for them and that we aren't paying attention to their performance because we have no interest in them for the role. I could be whispering to the suit, "Hey, this guy is perfect." Don't forget that if we are recording your performance we can watch it later. I know some women who will disagree with this, but I, as a male, can talk and listen at the same time! I can think of many times where we were whispering favorable things and the actor got very upset because he thought we weren't paying attention to his audition. Getting upset or copping an attitude will certainly put you in the "not cast" category.

If the director isn't nice to you in the audition, it may be because he spends his days "putting out fires" and dealing with massive egos from literally hundreds of people. This doesn't excuse being rude. I believe that everyone in an audition should treat each actor with dignity and respect. Most directors agree with me, but there are some who apparently don't.

You might find that people in your audition are eating pizza or pasta; don't let it upset you. I believe this is extremely rude, but this director or producer might be in the middle of a shoot and is seeing actors during his lunch hour. Again, if the audition is recorded, don't worry too much because they can watch the playbacks at a later time.

While we're discussing attitude, don't treat small roles as insignificant. They are significant to us; sometimes they are the hardest roles to cast. To cast a one or two line part is sometimes harder than a major role. Then again, don't treat that one line so importantly that you overplay it. We realize it's the most important line to you, but it's only secondary to the leads. Each part that we cast costs us a lot of money. One or two line parts aren't written into a script for any reason other than they are needed. Don't snub your nose at these roles while in an audition. When you know in advance that a small part is what you'll be auditioning for and you don't want such a part, fine, then don't come into the audition room.

Upstaging Your Fellow Actors

Don't come in bouncing off the walls. Actors do this to try to show up their partners standing next to them. They think that by talking constantly and joking with the actor(s) with whom they are reading they will stand out. Yeah, they'll stand out for sure! Have personality, but not at the expense of your fellow actors.

Directors may say differently in public, but privately no one wants to work with someone who is arrogant and down to ten brain cells.

For me, talking constantly without regard for your fellow actors puts you in this category.

I've already said that the entertainment communities of Los Angeles and New York are small; they are much smaller than people imagine. Be careful what you say and to whom you say it. You may want to unload on us in the audition room, but stick to the purpose of the audition—to help you obtain work. Saying negative things about anyone while in an audition will be counterproductive to your achieving that goal.

CHAPTER SIX

Don't Audition in Clothes that Would Embarrass the Family Doctor

For some reason the public sees us differently, but we are family people, too. We have children and do worry about the effects that our films have on them. For this reason, always dress appropriately in an audition.

Let me be more explicit. Unless a particular part calls for it, and there are relatively few that do, women, don't come into the audition wearing two Dixie cups and a Handi-Wipe. Too many women come wearing clothing that looks like something three silkworms turned out during their morning coffee break! It's amazing to us how many women in Los Angeles are practicing nudism on the installment plan.

Men, don't come in wearing tight, tight, tight, tight, tight jeans that make it appear as though you shoplifted a banana and two oranges. Your jeans are too tight if by just sitting down you qualify for joining the Vienna Boys' Choir.

If you have the incredible body of the futuristic Judy Jetson and were auditioning for a part which contained nudity, this might be an exception to the rule. Then you might want to wear clothes that appear as though they were thrown on with a pitchfork and it would be appropriate. Should nudity be involved, you must be notified (union rules) before your first audition for that particular role. This is what legitimate people do.

In regards to nudity, it is always your choice whether to audition for such a role or not. I have no real opinions here except to remind you that one day you might have a family. The project could be around for many years, even after your death.

What You Shouldn't Wear

Solid black, solid white or solid red are usually awful shirt colors to wear for an audition. There are exceptions, but this is a pretty basic rule. When light hits solid white, it causes a glow and really emphasizes the white. Many times what you see as solid white shirts on TV or film are a very light blue or light yellow. Those colors "soften" the white, but usually appear as white on camera.

During actual shoots, directors normally steer pretty clear of the white. One thing you learn as a director is, all else being equal, the eye will drift toward the lightest point of any picture. You don't want the eye drifting towards your shirt. You want it on your face. Aren't television and film known as the "home of the close-up?" And that close-up is usually on the face. It is why directors often refer to television as "talking heads."

Solid black appears too stark. It's especially bad for black-and-white photographs, for obvious reasons. And solid red really calls attention to itself on camera. I've heard policemen say that red cars stand out more than any other color of automobiles when they're looking at traffic.

Unless for some reason it would be beneficial for the role you're reading for, don't wear any silk clothes. Any clothes that shine are a no-no. They reflect too much light and take the focus off your face. Floral and paisley patterns also cause problems, so I would think twice before wearing them.

Costumes are a definite no-no. They are probably wrong for the part anyway. At some point the costume will draw our attention more than the actor. It is a definite distraction that you don't need in an audition.

Consider your accessories and don't wear expensive jewelry. When guys come in with Rolex watches (usually fake knock-offs) and gold chains, we're thinking, "This guy has a huge inheritance and doesn't need to make his living as an actor." This may sound offbeat, but if a part came down to two equally perfect people for a particular role, and one wore expensive jewelry and designer clothes and the other was dressed more modestly, we'd probably give it to the latter. That person could use the job and may be more appreciative. That may sound like a stretch, but there are good reasons for not going in as though you're the Clampetts, or as though you're the type that reads *Cosmopolitan* magazine and actually understands it, unless the part calls for that. And even then, keep it subtle.

I guess you could find an exception in some hemisphere if a part called for it, but guys shouldn't wear earrings. Forget the body piercing, too. Don't have rings in your nose, in your eyebrows, and a stud through your tongue that make it appear as though you fell face-first into a tackle box. You'll cut yourself out of many auditions if someone can hang a shower curtain from your cheeks.

Women, don't wear too much perfume, so that you leave the room before your perfume does and bloodhounds aren't needed to track you down. Men, don't overdo the "Evening at the L.A. Zoo" cologne, either. Some actors could make Right Guard turn left. I've had to air the room out many times in auditions. It slows us up and doesn't do much for your chances.

What You Should Wear

Here are my tips about what you should wear. For an audition for a TV show that is currently airing, be sure to watch as many episodes of that show as possible before the audition to see what the show's style is. Notice their wardrobe and how it fits in with the colors on the sets, and so forth. Notice what types of patterns the actors generally have in their clothes.

You have a real advantage for a currently running TV show. Even if you are not auditioning for a particular show, I'd start becoming familiar with the style of the TV shows that you do watch. You never know when you might get an audition for one before you'll have a chance to see more episodes.

If you're auditioning for a feature film or a TV show that isn't currently running, then get as much information as possible about the character for which you'll be reading. The information might not be accurate, as we'll discuss later, but still try to get every piece of information from your agent as possible.

Suggest the part with your wardrobe when you come into the audition; don't hit us over the head. For the part of a hillbilly you could come in wearing overalls. You don't have to come into the audition carrying a shotgun and waving a pitchfork. For a cowboy you could wear jeans and a western shirt. There's no need for the spurs, or to carry a saddle, or to lasso everyone in the office. Remember that the people who are "helping" the director make his decisions might not have much creative ability. Help them out, but don't overdo it!

If you're auditioning for a commercial, you have all kinds of ways to do research. In general, watch commercials so you begin to get the feel of the style each company uses. If you're auditioning for a Coca-Cola commercial, you might consider wearing shades of red and white. (Note: not *solid* red or *solid* white, for reasons previously discussed.)

By adopting that approach, the people watching you begin to associate you with the product. This may sound a bit out there, but it's true. Don't think I'm some Hollywood dude who might be medicated. (I'm Louisiana-born and have never taken an illicit drug in my life). You'd be surprised how many times people wearing colors of the product have come into auditions and I've heard someone in the room come out with words like, "Tom, he just reminds me of the product."

Now, don't take things to the extreme. I'm suggesting a beginning point and something to think about. The character you're reading for may look ridiculous in the product colors. Just take the colors into consideration.

Run down to your local supermarket and observe the actual product. Look at the packaging, the colors, and the designs. Are there any pictures of people on the packaging? Check out their hairstyles and their clothes. Those people were cast because they represented the product well; at least in someone's eyes. Don't take this to the extreme either; just use it as one of your reference tools.

Maybe you can actually visit the company that is doing the commercial. Is there a local branch of the bank whose commercial you're auditioning for? How about running down there and picking up some of their brochures? Their brochures were probably put together by the same ad agency that is shooting the commercial. And check websites. Most companies have them. Nowadays, you don't have to leave your residence to obtain information about the product for which you're auditioning.

For commercial auditions as opposed to theatrical auditions, it's okay to be assertive with your wardrobe, to a certain degree. Ad agency people are sometimes a few French fries short of a Happy Meal and need some nudging in this department. You can come in dressed pretty much the part and everyone will applaud you for it.

If it fits in with the character you're reading for, it is sometimes a good idea to come in dressed as you were in your photos, as it gives you more recognition. But only do this if it is appropriate for that particular role. After all, you were called in because of what someone "saw" in your photo.

Check with your agent to see if she knows what season it is supposed to be for that particular project, and where the project is supposedly located. This is especially true for commercials. In the heat of July you might be called in for a commercial audition that might be airing during the Christmas season. Having the information on locale and the season of the commercial will help you dress accordingly.

I constantly hear actors say they never get enough information about the roles they are reading for to accurately make wardrobe decisions. This may or may not be a legit complaint. Under the circumstances, use your noggin and come up with your own ways to research what attire would be appropriate for a particular character.

CHAPTER SEVEN

Don't Come into the Audition Playing the Part

I have totally changed my mind on this theory, which is ironic. Way back in history, when I was still an actor and Madam Butterfly was still a caterpillar, I had always been taught by acting teachers to show the director that you "are the part" by how you act before you actually read.

This advice made perfectly good sense to me and I followed it carefully. The idea behind this was that by acting as the character would act as soon as you enter the room, this would make the director think of you as the part in real life. Supposedly, this would give him more incentive to cast you. Wrong!

After sitting in only a few auditions as a director, I quickly learned that practicing this theory had been a huge mistake. Actors think they are being unique by acting like the part in real life before their reading, but everyone in the audition room sees through you doing this. Never forget that you're only one of hundreds of actors we're seeing for that part on that day alone.

Let us suppose you're playing the part of the type of person that goes to a horror movie and roots for the monster. You come into the audition room being mean to everyone, making us think we'd be safer in the electric chair than sitting there with you. Actors have actually come into the audition being harsh and sometimes even cussing at us to show us that they are this mean person in real life.

Do you believe we're thinking, "Wow, he's perfect for the part.... He's really a jerk"? Or do you believe we're thinking, "Wow, he's just a jerk"? You can bet it's the latter. You're doing what just about every other actor is doing—acting like a jerk to us. At some point the client will turn to me and say, "Are actors jerks or what?"

Another reason you shouldn't come into the audition as the character is, we will probably change the character during the audition process. If you play as a jerk, we might think that is all you can play, since you are one in real life. What happens if we modify the character and don't want him as jerky anymore and we think that jerky is all you can do? For the same reason, you shouldn't "slate" (the stating of your name on camera) in character, either. I know a lot of acting instructors tell you to do this, but for the above reasons and many more, it's a bad idea. You really don't know what we're looking for anyway, since we're not sure ourselves at that point in the audition process.

I know you've watched TV talk shows where actors have stated that they came into auditions playing the part. And since most actors do this, the odds are that we might cast someone who came in acting the part. However, I submit that if you just come in as yourself and then play the part, you are showing us much more versatility as an actor. Coming in with one personality and then totally altering your personality for the actual reading is quite impressive.

I'm not saying you can't take some of your natural traits that could also be used when playing the part, but be careful, and think twice about playing the part as you walk in the door. Don't overemphasize it. We're casting the actor, not the person, so don't be on stage and perform during the chitchat session.

It's not a good idea to come in using an accent or dialect that you believe is right for the part before you start your reading, unless it is native to you. Usually it comes off as being very phony. I would be extremely careful about adding an accent or dialect that isn't part of the character. There are a few occasions where I'm sure something like this has worked.

Is this to say, then, that you should come in and act differently than the character even if the character is the same as you? No! Either way, come in as yourself!

Taking Direction

Be extremely careful not to become too set on how you want to play the part before you walk into the audition room. Many actors become so engrossed in how they think the part should be played that it becomes the only way they can play it.

Directors like to know that actors can take direction. Many times a director will give you direction to play the part differently, even if you nailed the part the first time. Perhaps you come in and have to play a scene in which you become very angry. You really nailed it and the director is incredibly impressed. Still, he might give you direction not to play it so mean and try to warm the character up. His request doesn't necessarily mean that for the actual shoot he wants the character warmed up, but merely that he is trying to see how well you do or don't take direction.

If you disagree with the director's direction in an audition, don't argue with him. I just said, the director might not actually want the character played this new way in the actual shoot. The audition isn't the place for actors to show their knowledge of, or lack thereof, the character by getting into a heavy discussion with the director about that character or the script. This is a great way to talk yourself right out of an acting job.

By all means let the director direct. You never know what's going on with the suits. Maybe this is the first chance the director has to exercise some power with the suits; he's trying to show the suits that he can direct. Personally, I would never use an actor's audition to do this, but I know directors who do.

Going back to the director's request, if you're very set in the way you had been practicing the character you might be unable to warm that character up. This tells the director one of two things: Either you weren't listening, a big no-no, or you have no range as an actor. Both are equally bad and very disturbing to a director.

You happen to do anger very well, but calm, "talkie" scenes are not your bag. This is why we give direction. If you weren't listening and you do it the same way, you would be in the majority of actors. Actors are nervous and start to nod knowingly immediately after we start talking.

Bottom Line: Listen to what the director tells you. He is testing your ability to take direction.

If you don't understand some direction given to you in an audition, then ask for clarification. That's not the same as asking how to play a part. It is simply trying to understand direction given to you. Producers, especially, sometimes give confusing direction from time to time. Sometimes their message is floating in a bottle somewhere in the Mediterranean. It is perfectly acceptable, and even advisable, to ask for clarification if you are confused by our direction.

Don't come into the audition trying to impress on us that you need a moment to "get into character." We're not *im*pressed. In fact, we are *de*pressed. All the director is thinking about is the money you're going to cost him on the set by needing all of this extra time. If you need extra time, arrive at the audition a little earlier than the rest of the crowd. Then you can go into the restroom and perform mirror exercises, or whatever it takes for you to get into character.

I'm not putting any kind of method down in any way here. Many of the acting methods are very helpful and you should study every type of acting method and non-method. But don't think we're excited about you taking a few moments to get into character, as you learned in your acting classes. We see it as a case of actors trying to be "artsy."

I was directing a food commercial when an actor came into the audition and said he needed five minutes to "think like a French fry; I need to 'see' the French fry; I need to 'taste' the French fry; and I need to 'experience' the French fry." He mentioned that he learned to do this prep work while studying acting in college. My feeling is, the only Preparation he got there was "H." All he had to say was, "um, um." Sorry, we weren't doing Shakespeare; we were selling French fries!

Don't Play the Extremes

Please, don't come in playing some extreme character, unless the part really calls for it. Just play the character honestly. Film and television "ain't" stage acting. Stage actors auditioning for film and TV need to remember to play these characters as real. Unless you're doing some weird show, or possibly some children's character-type show, you're pretty much going to play your age and type. We're not going to put white shoe polish in your hair so that you can play a part thirty years your senior. We would just get someone thirty years older. This isn't the high-school play where we have a limited age range from which to choose. In theatre this might be done sometimes, but with the close-ups on camera this rarely happens.

This isn't to say that you can't take risks with the character, meaning trying something different with it than is apparent in the script. Just don't take such a large risk that you become unbelievable and work your way right out of a job. Keep it believable!

Usually, you can take bigger risks when auditioning for the stage. Since the stage audience is much further away than the screen audience, bigger can sometimes become better.

Getting Personal

While you're playing your part, please don't touch us. Some actors doing a scene where they are supposed to be very mean, will not only act mean to us, but they might get physical to show how mean they can really be. I've been kicked, scratched, yanked, socked, and pushed by actors trying to show us how they can really play the part to the max. Casting directors usually have the most interactions with the actors because they're the ones usually reading with them. You can be assured that they don't want you to get physical with them.

Even if the scene calls for it, don't fondle the casting director or anyone in an audition for that matter. Don't kiss them, either. Keep in mind how many actors we're seeing for these parts. I've seen actors put their hands up the casting director's skirt! Please! You only embarrass the casting director and us when you perform such nonsense.

When you get personal with someone in the room, it is unusual that they are informed of it in advance. So it shocks and distracts them, and us, from your audition. Then we're concentrating on the shocking incident and not your reading.

It's not necessary to pick up objects from our desks and use them while you're in character. I've had things hurled off my desk, objects thrown across the room, plants knocked over, guns pointed at my head, and more. My mug has been taken off my desk and used as a prop. Basically, don't use our things, or us, as props. In fact, don't use props in an audition unless we provide them. When actors come in with props, you look as though you're still on the stage doing a theatrical performance. If props are needed for a stage or screen audition, they will be provided.

Don't pantomime picking up objects, either. An exception might be in a scene where you need to talk on the phone and none is available; then pantomiming would be okay. Yes, many acting classes teach you how to pick up objects that aren't really there, but that's just what they are—acting classes, not auditions.

Playing Your Personality

You don't have to be a brilliant actor to work in this industry, especially with regards to the screen medium. You can turn on TV any day or night, or go to the movie theatres, and catch yourself thinking, "How did that person ever get an acting job?" I know, I say it to myself all the time. I've said it to myself during actual filming! Not having to be brilliant doesn't mean there shouldn't at least be something very interesting about you.

You don't have to be of the glamorous type, either. There's acting work for your type even if you can make roadkill get up and walk away or your hourglass figure is "way past noon." There is much more work for character actors than model types.

To illustrate, let's move this discussion to the music business. You don't have to be a great singer to sell records. There's no big revelation here! How many times do you think to yourself, "How did this person ever get a record deal?" The record company doesn't wonder. They realize that the reason their recording stars are superstars is because they have that one very important ingredient—Personality!

Neil Diamond is one of my favorite singers. I'm being honest when I admit that Neil is not the greatest singer in the world. Does it matter? Not really! He has a certain style, or personality, with which people connect. He happens to have sold millions of albums and CDs.

One of my all-time favorite songs is "Maggie May," by Rod Stewart. No one has ever accused Rod Stewart of being the greatest singer in the world, either. But it really doesn't matter because his style and personality connect with the public; hence his success for so many years.

Years ago I happened to catch a performance given by Bob Dylan. If Bob hits a note, it's a coincidence. But you know what? I'm as crazy about his music as are thousands of other fans. He has been extremely successful for years. The point is, you don't have to be a brilliant singer to sell CDs, but you do have to have an interesting personality.

I could go on about singers, such as Madonna whose phenomenal success has little to do with vocal ability. It's all about "Personality." Many singers who are better are never heard about and never will be.

We can equate this illustration with the acting profession. I'm a big Squint Eastwood fan. Never mind that he doesn't play a huge variety of characters. Pretty much Squint walks the same, talks the same, delivers most lines the same, and even squints the same, but how can you not like Squint? His character works well for him and he, rightfully, continues to play that very believable character. We can think of

John Wayne who played "John Wayne" in almost every film that John Wayne performed in. Yet John Wayne will go down as one of our greatest and best-loved actors of all time. And what about Jack Nicholson who is "Jack Nicholson" in most of his films? He does a great job, but it is usually as "Jack." Millions of people, including me, love his work and his films.

One of my favorite actors is of the lesser talented variety as far as acting is concerned. I'm crazy about this woman—Dolly Parton (I'm not crazy about her for those two reasons!). No matter what Dolly does, you just like Dolly. Nor was George Burns the greatest actor of all time. When George Burns played God, he played "George Burns." When George Burns played the devil, he played "George Burns." And when George Burns played "George Burns," he played "George Burns." But how can you not like George Burns? Not many film and TV stars play a wide variety of characters.

My comments are not a put-down to these successful people by any stretch of the imagination. The opposite is true. Many screen actors have found a personality and/or character that works for them and they have been very successful at their craft. Finding this character is often what separates the working from the non-working actor. "Typecasting," you mention? Yes, but notice that the key word in "typecast" is "cast."

The "Purist" Actor

The actors who we call "purists" (actors who are artsy) will cringe at the previous section. Fine, cringe. If it makes the purists feel any better, my entire background before entering the screen world was as an actor in the theatre for 15 years. I love the theatre. But let's face it, there's no money in Shakespeare; there's lots of money in French fries.

Directors and producers also get typecast to the same degree. "Oh, that director only does comedy." "That producer has only produced drama." Does this mean that these people are incapable of working on other types of projects? Absolutely not, but we get the same thing said about us as actors do when it comes to typecasting

Years ago, for six weeks every year, I was an instructor for the graduating class at the American Academy of Dramatic Arts, West. I was an actor at the time. An artsy instructor there would belittle me in his classes because I had sold out as an actor simply because I had a recurring role on the daytime drama, *General Hospital*. He mentioned to his class one day that in television, "People just play themselves.... What kind of acting is that?"

Later I could no longer teach at the Academy because I was just beginning my directing career, while still performing the recurring role I had on *General Hospital*. I ran into that instructor on the set of the soap where he had an "Under Five," which means that an actor is not a principal player or an extra, but in-between with under five lines. (I'll discuss this later.) He saw me and was somewhat embarrassed since he had apparently sold out for a much smaller role than he had ridiculed me for. I got some satisfaction out of the incident since his two lines were delivered to me. To you artsy types, most actors will grab at the chance to work in the "selling out" markets, given the opportunity.

There is nothing wrong with using your personality in your characters. Purists will say you totally become the character—Hogwash! There has to be some of you in your characters. If everyone just "played the character," there would be no reason to see a multitude of actors audition for Hamlet. All they would need would be to "become" Hamlet with their interpretations exactly the same. This is impossible.

So, you don't have to come in "playing the part" before you audition, and you certainly don't have to play the part in any particular way during your reading. There is no right or wrong way to play a part, although some ways are definitely better than other ways. But there's no direct right or wrong way to play any particular character.

One thing I've learned over the years is that in an audition, if I'm seeing two hundred people in one day, I will see two hundred different interpretations of that character that day. We're all thankful for that. If everyone played it exactly the same, we wouldn't need auditions; we'd just find the person who physically fit the role and cast him.

Bottom line: Just be yourself in the audition, especially during the chitchat session. If you aren't yourself in the chitchat session because you are posing, sooner or later you'll forget the pose, and then you'll appear phony. With regards to your reading, there is nothing wrong with using part of your personality to help you with the character. It is very advantageous.

CHAPTER EIGHT
Don't Get Too Nervous

Okay, you've been with me up to this point, but this one is impossible! Not really. A little nervousness is fine. In fact, a little nervousness gives you energy and can be helpful. We directors are probably more nervous in an audition than you are! I bite my nails so much that my stomach needs a manicure.

I realize asking an actor how he feels about auditioning is like asking a lamppost how it feels about dogs. Auditioning imposes a mental torture that only algebra has a right to inflict, but you have nothing to lose and everything to gain on an audition. Admittedly, you don't have the part yet, and odds are you probably won't get the part, but the director does have his job and people are expecting him to perform his duties, and perform them well. One bad casting decision can ruin an entire show. You could say, we're in worse shape than you are.

Another person who is nervous in an audition is the casting director—probably more nervous than the director. Why? Because this casting director told us you were perfect for the part. If you don't do a good job in the audition, it makes us question the casting director's judgment. They are really putting their reputations on the line with each actor they send to the director and producer. Perhaps because everyone in the audition room has a lot at stake and is somewhat apprehensive during the audition process, this thought will help you relax.

Some actors enter an audition more nervous than a tree in a Benji movie. They'll say, "I'm a little nervous. . . . I haven't done this very much. . . . I'm just getting started." Imagine applicants to be a pilot telling potential employers how nervous they were about flying an airplane. The same goes for surgeons, or any other professional for that matter.

We *are* on your side. When you're auditioning you are the most important person in the audition room. We're there for you. Why wouldn't we want you to be anything but great? We need you more than you need us at this point. We already have our jobs, so we actually don't matter as much as you at that moment.

So, I'll say it again, "Relax." You answer, "Right." You've psyched yourself up to get nervous. I think I can talk you out of it.

Why You Get Nervous

I believe there are three major reasons why actors become so nervous in auditions. All of them are mentally created. One, you get nervous because you're worried that you're going to make a fool out of yourself. You are! Everyone does. Please don't think you are unique and that you're the only person who's going to make a fool of himself. Hey, it's better to make a fool of yourself than to make nothing of yourself. We cast fools all the time! But don't worry, because as time goes on and you begin to master the art of auditioning, you'll start making a fool of yourself in a more dignified manner.

Since everyone makes a fool of himself on an audition, just accept the fact that you're going to also, and move on. After that recognition, there's no longer any reason to worry. I don't mean that you become so engrossed in this point that you become victim to the Beverly Theory, either. I'm just saying that you should accept the fact that everyone makes a fool of himself in an audition. And whether you've accepted this fact or not, it's true, so let's move on. Just realize that an audition is a special time you've set aside to humiliate yourself.

To make you feel better, let me confirm something that you may already have heard: It really doesn't matter if you make a fool of yourself in some high-level advertising executive's office, for example. He probably won't have his job in six months anyway, because the turnover in that business is unbelievable. So quit worrying. There is one very important exception here: Casting directors do hang around for a long time, so you don't want to make a bad impression with any of them.

The second reason for nervousness in auditions is because actors think, erroneously, they have a real good chance of getting this particular part. Who are you kidding? The odds of your getting this particular part are so low that it's not worth getting nervous over. Consider your chances as fat or slim. (Isn't it odd that they have the same meaning?) Since you have now accepted the fact that you're probably not going to get this particular part, you don't have to worry about that anymore.

Forget getting the job. Actors come out of auditions saying, "I lost the job." Wrong! You can't lose something you never had. I don't mean to have a defeatist attitude—quite the contrary. Think back to all the times that you took tests in school, when you were relaxed and it didn't really matter whether you made a good grade or not on a particular test. Probably these were the times you made the best grades. Actors take a particular audition too seriously. While you should take your work very seriously, don't take this particular audition so seriously that you think this job will make your career. Being aware that you probably aren't going to get the job anyway, go into the audition, make a friend and have a good time. Be like a guy going out on a first date with the woman of his dreams. She informs you right off there's no way you're going to get a good-night kiss, or whatever. You know what? You're almost relieved! The pressure is off. You've accepted that nothing's going to happen, you're comfortable with that, and it's no longer worth worrying about.

I mentioned in Chapter Seven that acting teachers instruct their students to start believing they have the part as they're sitting in the lobby waiting to audition. They rationalize that the actor will walk in with a very positive attitude. No one believes in a positive attitude more than I do. You are, however, setting yourself up for disappointment. The odds of your getting the part are too slim for you to believe otherwise. But I'm not saying you should walk in negatively, setting up a self-fulfilling prophecy (i.e., Beverly Theory). Absolutely not! You're an upbeat actor. Yes, you're going to have a positive attitude about your future in this business. You accept that you will eventually get work and become a successfully working actor. You realize that you're a better actor than most of your competition. I'm only saying that the odds of your getting this one particular part don't justify all the wasted energy on being so nervous.

If I told you up-front that you were physically wrong for this part and there's no way I could cast you, but that you could read anyway, you would probably give your best reading. The pressure is off because the fantasy, "I have a good chance of getting this role," has been taken off the table.

In the same way, showing up for an audition, you see hundreds of actors lined up for four blocks that are reading for the same part as you. You look at them all and think to yourself, "What a joke!" Your nervousness just goes zip because you realize that the odds of your getting this part over all of these others are extremely remote. You know what? We are seeing that many people over the course of the day. Maybe not when you happen to arrive at the audition, but we are seeing that many people.

Have you ever interviewed for a non-acting job that you really didn't want and had decided that you weren't going to take even if it was offered? Wasn't that the job you got? You got it because you didn't overplay your cards in the interview; you didn't come off as being desperate.

Is the Room Full of Experts?

My third, and main, reason for believing actors get nervous in auditions is they think that they are walking into a room full of experts on acting. You couldn't be further from the truth. You probably know more about acting than everyone in the room—combined! If you're a serious actor you've been studying acting daily for years.

These guys haven't. If you haven't been studying acting regularly, you should have been; your competition has!

Back in the eighties when there was more hair on my head than in my ears, I taught an acting class for all three of the major networks. Actors had to have their own TV series just to be in the class. If the actor's show was in reruns, the networks didn't want their actors sitting around for three months not working on their craft. So, unless they are acting in some other project during their off time, the networks want their actors to keep studying their craft.

I can't urge you enough to take acting class after acting class. I find that the actors who are working the most continue to study no matter how successful they become. Many name actors who you see in films and on television shows are in acting classes at this very moment. You might get lucky and obtain an acting job in a TV series or film, but to sustain a career you really need to know your craft.

To illustrate my point, I'm going to give you a few, admittedly extreme, examples of what happens in auditions. I say few, because in the university lectures I give, I spend about five hours solely on examples of how little the people in the audition room know about actors. Keep in mind that I, the director, usually make final casting decisions. My examples are ones where I didn't have that power.

Legal reasons prevent me from mentioning the actual names of products or films and television shows involved. The first example concerns an audition for a major soft drink company. This woman came in and gave one of the best auditions I've ever seen in my life. Not only did she nail that audition, she was incredibly beautiful. Her features knew the importance of teamwork.

I have a little routine I go through in front of the client after an actor I really like leaves the audition room where I jump up and down, point towards the door, and give this huge smile. This client observed my routine, turned to me and said, "You want her?"

"Absolutely! She is perfect," I replied.

"Can't use her," he shot back.

"I don't understand.... She looks great, reads well, and is physically exactly what we talked about," I stated.

He looked at me very matter-of-factly and said, "She looks like my ex-wife, Satan's sister, and I can't stand that twit." He obviously had a bad brains-to-testosterone ratio.

The decision had nothing to do with the actor's ability. Yet she did what all actors do when they arrive home from an audition and don't receive a callback. She went through what I call "the actor's routine."

On her way home from the audition, she would have run through this mental routine. Anyone who has not received a callback after an audition has gone through some form of this routine in their head. It goes something like this: "You know, I could've gone in there and been a little meaner in that one part.... I should've worn that other shirt.... Why didn't I get there earlier?"

"I could have.... I should have.... Why didn't I....?" You get the point. She'll beat herself up because that's what actors do after an audition, however well they read.

During another audition for a network TV show to be sponsored by a major soap company, this girl came in and gave a wonderful reading, again nailing the audition. Besides which, she had the perfect hair color to complement the shampoo for the commercials the soap company was going to air during the show. She walked out the door and I went through my little physical routine. Then came the usual response when the client disagreed. "You want her?" he asked.

"Oh, yeah. She's perfect. What a talent!" I remarked confidently.

He shot back, "We can't use her. She doesn't use Balsam, Balsam." ("Balsam, Balsam" is my generic name for his company's shampoo.)

At first I thought he was joking and waited for a punch line. I couldn't imagine a client would dump an actor just because he believed she didn't use his company's shampoo. When no punch line was forthcoming, I shot back with a little sarcasm, "I'll tell you what we're gonna do. I will send a hair-and-makeup person to her house every day. And every day that she arrives on our set her hair will have been washed with Balsam, Balsam, okay?"

"Tom, you just really don't get it, do you?"

"Not really. What's the problem?"

"She doesn't use it on a regular basis, you know," he stupidly re-marked.

First of all, how did he know that? Second, who cares? And third, what difference would it have made? The role was for the part of a prostitute. I sat there wondering if he was stupid or a Cuban had hi-jacked his brain. Maybe he had ridden the Tilt-a-Whirl too long.

But you know what that actor did when she got home? Yes, she would have gone through the actor's routine: "I could have . . . . I should have . . . . Why didn't I . . . . ?" Again, it had nothing to do with her performance, but I'll bet she went home and beat herself up be-cause that's what actors do after an audition. After about ten auditions and going home and performing the actor's routine each time, she'll start coming into auditions a little more nervous, a little more scared, and a little more apologetic. All the characteristics that start actors spi-raling downward as far as nervousness and apologies are concerned.

Example three is taken from a feature film audition, which was being held at one of the biggest movie studios in Hollywood. Think of film shown on a movie screen as being dozens upon dozens of times larger than real life. If I shoot a close-up of your face where there is a pimple, and then put that close-up on the big screen, that pimple would be the size of two six-foot-tall people standing on top of each other! That's a twelve-foot circumference! So in film audi-tions we're looking for "less."

A woman was auditioning with another actor. She began her reading while doing this ridiculous interpretive dance. (I learned later that she was a prima ballerina.) Very loudly she said to the actor, "Agoneee, in Agoneee, I looooooooove you."

Her performance was not just over the top, it was way, way, way over the top. Not only was her performance Broadway style, but she wasn't even reading what was written on my script. So I was beginning to think that she was in the wrong audition, that the *Twilight Zone* was probably auditioning down the hallway. Then I wondered whether the studio sent her in as a plant to test my stress levels. Finally, in this short period of time, I realized that perhaps she was "dating" the guy sitting next to me. This happens in auditions. Therefore, I didn't want to hint that I was stunned with the dancing routine and the worst overacting I had ever seen.

So, I politely asked her to start over. Unfortunately, she did. After she repeated her insane little dance, she shouted, "Agoneee, in Agoneee, I looooooooove you."

Uh-oh, there she goes again. Since I didn't see this "Agoneee" character in my script, I asked to see her script to find out what was going on. She handed me her script and I was stunned to find that it was a photocopy of the script I had.

A few moments later I figured things out. Before the words, "I love you" that she was supposed to say, there was a parenthetical stage direction as to how to deliver the line, stating "(Agony, in agony)." She was to say, "I love you," in agony, but she thought the script named that actor "Agony," and called him that.

As she was leaving the audition I was mentally comparing her to Venus de Milo—beautiful, but not all there. I concluded there was too much chlorine in her gene pool. With regards to conception, it's hard to believe that she beat out a million other sperm.

I didn't know what to say to the suit sitting next to me. By now, I had learned my lesson about saying anything too negative about anyone in an audition. I decided that I would comment in a very neutral way, playing it right down the middle to confuse the suit.

"Unbelievable," I said matter-of-factly, with no commitment either positive or negative. He said, "Unbelievable."

From the way he said the word, I didn't get either a positive or a negative reading, so I decided to try again. "Wow," I blurted out. He retorted with a slight whisper, "Wooooooooooooow," which I didn't like the sound of. But I didn't want to jump to any conclusions, so I decided to try one more time.

Staring right at him, I said "Wooooooooo." He said, "Wooooooooo, let me tell you something about that actor."

I smartly said, "What?"

"This 'Agoneee' thing shows how vulnerable that actor really is," he retorted.

"No, it shows how stupid she really is," I responded.

"No, it shows how much vulnerability she has," he replied.

"No, it shows how much stupidity she has," I shot back.

You guessed it, even though she was obviously suffering from permanent beach damage with an IQ at about room temperature, he cast her right over my head. I had no decision. She is now on the editing room floor and the footage will never be seen again.

In another audition, I was looking for a woman to play the girlfriend of a pretty major star. In advance, one of the suits came to me and said, "You know, our star isn't really that good of an actor so you can't cast anyone who will upstage him. She can't be better looking than him, or a better actor."

Their thought process went like this: If you have an actor who isn't so great and he's the star, surround him with actors that are worse so the star will look better. Huh? I disagree vehemently with this idea when it comes to actors, but I kind of understood their thought process. When I was in the eighth grade I wanted to stand out as being good-looking, so I mingled with ugly people.

An actor should always do his best, but you should know that some people have lost acting jobs because they were too good at their craft. It's extremely rare, so always do your best. I'm trying to show you that casting is a strange process that no one really understands, so quit becoming overly nervous about it.

An actor came in to read for the girlfriend of the star. She was fabulous; she read great; she looked perfect for the part. I went into my little dance routine in her support, at which point the suit turned to me and said there was no way we could use her because her hair was distracting and that she would upstage our star. It was true that she had that kind of model hairdo that looks as though it has been arranged in front of an airplane propeller, or that a pardon has come through ten seconds after they pulled the switch. In other words, that the hair has been combed with an eggbeater.

I said, "I realize her hair is having an electrical storm, but . . . . "

"Tom, I didn't say 'her hair' was distracting, I said 'that hair' is distracting."

"Huh," I cleverly replied.

"Tom, did you look at her left eyebrow?"

"Ah, I looked at her face but I didn't zoom in on a particular eyebrow."

"Well, perhaps you should have. She had this long hair sticking up on her left eyebrow and it's distracting," he said with authority.

I made my fingers look like scissors and opened and closed the fingers next to my left eyebrow to show cutting. A moment later he said, "We don't wanna do that. It'll just grow back." Obviously, his antenna wasn't picking up all the channels.

I've used extreme situations as examples. For your peace of mind, many times there are very professional people who are auditioning you. I'm not trying to state differently. But I do see lesser degrees of the extreme examples all the time in auditions. I'm stating here that you can only do the best you can, even if someone in the room has an intelligence problem and doesn't have his belt through all the loops. Always remain the expert on acting while in the audition. That doesn't mean be cocky; it means be confident that you know your craft.

Owing Favors

Discussing your misplaced nervousness about your audition, let me take things a step further. You may lose a part because the director owes a favor, as I pointed out briefly in Chapter Three. Perhaps I landed a directing job through someone and I need to pay him back. He asks that his son read for a certain part and that he "hopes I will pay special attention to him." "Well, this is really unfair," you're thinking. Let's go back to what I've already stated: This is not a fair business—never has been, never will be. I, and other directors, receive all kinds of requests for favors from studio people, producers, and on, and on.

We also do other favors. Let's suppose the role comes down to two people, equally adept and both physically perfect for the part. The decision might come down to something as simple as which agent do I "owe." Maybe one of the agents of the two helped me secure a major star in the past. Maybe I can get one of that agent's stars if I hire a few of his lesser-known actors. This happens on a more frequent basis than you would imagine. It might be that we personally know one agent better than the other.

I first learned about the strange things that go on when an actor leaves the audition room way back when I was an actor. I used to bring my briefcase into every audition; inside it I had a tape recorder running, which would secretly record my audition. I thought this would help me for future auditions, since afterwards I would listen to the chitchat session I'd had with everyone and play back my actual reading.

I'd done this for a few years, until one time I left the briefcase in the audition room by mistake. I was halfway home before I realized what I had done and had to go back to retrieve it. I simply explained to the secretary in the lobby my forgetfulness and asked her to retrieve the briefcase for me, which she did.

On the way home, I played the tape back and got an earful. Not only did I hear my audition, but since the tape was still running after I had left, I also heard some of the ridiculous comments about my hair color and ears. From then on, I used the briefcase-forgetting routine, as long as I wasn't reading for the same people, and learned, even before becoming a director, that it might not always be the reading that gets an actor the part. I heard some bizarre things in those days, and now from the other side of the table I continue to hear bizarre things about performances from the suits. I can't recommend you do the above, because since then this routine was used on a *Seinfeld* episode.

Stars themselves have even told me that I was not to cast anyone who was better looking than they were. Maybe the star doesn't want to be upstaged. Or you look too much like the star of the film/TV show, or you resemble some other star too closely.

Another reason might be, we already have the star and you don't "physically fit" (known as "matching") with that particular star.

I could go on about what happens in auditions. I have enough material on this subject alone to fill an entire book. But let it suffice to say people are not cast for so many reasons. Beating yourself up when you don't get called back isn't worth it.

The Importance of Training

All of this, of course, does not negate the importance of you becoming the best actor possible. I regularly hear actors say, "People have told me I'm a natural." Yeah? Well, try being natural at four in the morning with three hundred crew members watching, while we change the script by the minute and start rearranging what scenes we're going to shoot all day long. Acting natural in real life doesn't really come into play here.

Stars take acting classes. I mentioned in Chapter One that I used to teach an acting class that was funded by the major networks and was set up just for stars who had their own TV series. The actors in that class had been doing their shows for years but were still in training.

All professionals go on learning. Doctors have to learn about new medicines and attend medical conventions. Attorneys continue to learn new case laws. Teachers take refresher courses. The FAA requires airline pilots to have additional training every six months. Get the point?

It's very important that you take acting classes to learn to act, not just to meet people. I mention that, because acting classes are a great place to meet people and network. Other actors will usually share information with you about roles they've heard about that you might be right for. And eventually, you'll probably be seen by industry people while in an acting class.

These classes help you to find your strengths and weaknesses as an actor. Learning this will guide your choice of which scenes to use and not to use as audition showcases; and in auditions, on your choice of how to perform certain types of material. Don't be too busy learning the tricks of the trade to miss learning the trade.

Most actors get depressed when they're not acting, so acting classes are important because they give you a chance to act! You're not only oiling your machine, you're relieving some of the stresses actors have when they don't get to act. When you're in an audition you don't want to show depression.

We'll discuss later "showcases" and "industry night" workshops, which you do take to meet industry people. But these don't substitute for most acting classes that should be taken for the purpose of learning. Take acting classes from as many different instructors as possible. They all have something to offer. Realize though, that just because the teacher has a big title next to his name, it has nothing to do with whether he can teach. Some of the many casting directors who teach classes are excellent; some teach to support themselves between jobs. I see nothing inherently wrong with this. And it really doesn't matter if the teacher is in a one-room studio in West Covina, or a major school in Los Angeles. The point is to learn your craft and to keep studying.

If you can find a good class with a screen director, definitely consider taking it. But be careful about instructors who advertise as "directors." Most instructors who use the "director" credential mislead actors who are taking film and TV and/or commercial acting classes.

Many times these instructors who are teaching screen acting classes have only directed plays, which is fine, but they have never directed for the screen. So don't assume anything.

To check whether a director has really directed anything for the screen, go to the Directors Guild of America website (www.dga.org) and see who is and who isn't a member. It is possible for someone to have directed low-budget projects that weren't under the Guild, but if a director is a DGA member, then you can consider him a real director. Just verify that he's listed under the "Director" category and not "Production Manager" or "Assistant Director" category. You can also go to the previously mentioned IMDB site (Internet Movie Database—www.imdb.com) and find out who has directed what, because it covers people who aren't members of the DGA, as well.

Do your research when it comes to finding acting instructors. Some of the training in Los Angeles isn't that great. Because no credentials are needed, anyone can hang out a shingle with "acting instructor" next to his name. If you find an acting class that sounds interesting, audit the class first. If they won't let you do that, it doesn't necessarily mean that the teacher isn't good. You can sit outside the class of a teacher who has a great reputation but doesn't allow auditing, and ask actors who leave the class what they think of it. When it comes to choosing acting classes, actors are usually your best source of information in this industry.

Things are different in New York than Los Angeles. New York actors tend to do more training. In New York actors spend their time working out in the theater. In Los Angeles actors spend their time working out in the gym. Mind you, there's nothing wrong with working out in the gym. In fact, I recommend it. However, you should spend lots of time on your craft as well.

Training will help keep your nervousness to a minimum, because it will give you more confidence. The better trained you are and the more confidence you have, the less likely you will be overly nervous in the audition.

The "Waiting Room" Competition

As if you aren't nervous enough, people will try to "psych" you out in the audition waiting room. They'll go on and on about all the parts they've turned down; they'll talk about the "new HBO contract" they just signed. (They're probably getting it for about $29.95 a month!) Don't listen to their Nazi psychological games and don't star in their psychodrama. They're probably doing no more acting work than you are. Study your part and don't pay any attention to the psycho-babble in the lobby. Just for fun we sometimes peek into the waiting room just to listen to the nonsense.

While we're speaking about lobby babble, please don't get caught up in the loud chatter. I can't tell you how many times in auditions we've had to send someone out into the lobby to hush the actors, because it sounded as though there was a bowling alley out there. You're being rude to your fellow actors.

Reality Check

What is the worst thing that can happen to you on an audition? Making a fool of yourself? No! As we discussed, everyone does. Being embarrassed? No! Everyone is. Breaking down in tears because your reading was so awful? No, that actually happens on occasion. Then what is the worst thing?

The worst thing is that you don't get the part. But haven't you already accepted that you're probably not going to get it anyway? So what's the loss? You didn't have the job when you walked in the door, so you really haven't lost anything, have you?

It's a fact that no matter how good or bad you are on an audition, someone on that audition likely will do better than you and someone will do worse. The worst person probably won't get the role and the best person might not get the role either. Accept that you aren't going to be perfect on every audition. (I said *accept* it—don't worry about it.) You will give some good auditions and you'll give others that'll leave a lot to be desired. And no matter how terrible you think a particular situation is, it can only become worse if you play into the Beverly Theory and the "actor's routine."

You might be surprised to learn that no matter how awful you were, someone in that room thought you were great. And vice versa—that no matter how great you were, someone thought you were awful. Half of the people in the room take notes and the other half take naps. Of eight people watching your playback, let me tell you what will happen: If you were great, three people will think you were awful, three will think you were terrific, and two won't give a damn. And the reverse: No matter how awful you were, three will think you were great, three will think you were awful, and two won't give a damn. I'm oversimplifying, obviously. But what I say has some truth to it and will keep you from driving yourself nuts.

I emphasize the importance of studying acting and becoming the best that you possibly can at your craft. In spite of all my comments, I don't want to give a wrong impression, because in the long run the better trained you are, the better off you're likely to be over the span of your career. I'm just saying that in this one particular audition that you happen to be in at this very moment, quit worrying about how good or bad you were.

In casting, there are just too many factors involved to make judgments about how you did in an audition based on whether you were called back or not. To a director, one particular role is but one piece of a very large and complex puzzle that he has to make fit; your ability as an actor is but one, although a very important factor.

Finally, look at this way: If we saw 400 people for the particular role you were auditioning for, does that mean that the 399 actors who didn't get the job weren't talented enough?

PART TWO
The Do's

CHAPTER NINE

Do Get Professional Photos

If you recall, in the introduction I said that I record every comment that every person in the audition room makes about each actor. Then, every evening I enter that data into a computer. It's from that information that I've based this chapter, as well as others—upon the opinions of thousands of directors and producers with, obviously, some of my own interpretation.

What Is the Purpose of a Photo (to a Director)?

Is there a different purpose of the photo to a director than there is to an agent or to a casting director? Think before you answer.

"To show them what types of characters I can play," is how most actors' respond. Not a bad answer, if the photo is for the purpose of obtaining an agent. But for a director, it's not the main purpose.

For a director, the main purpose of an actor's photo is "identification." For every ten people that I want to call back, I can't find a few of them because they don't resemble their photos. Yes, a director does look at the photo to see how light affects your face, how your features will photograph, and so forth. But your photo's immediate and main purpose in the actual audition is identification. Not looking like your photo is the number one complaint that pops up in my computer with regards to actors' photos.

You're probably wondering why we don't just play back your recorded audition if we can't find you and you seem to have joined the witness protection program. To help us make decisions, we may play it back, but it's rare to play back the entire audition tape just to identify someone. It takes a lot of time, which we usually don't have, so the odds of this happening are very slim. Besides, although most commercial auditions are recorded, many auditions for television and film roles are not.

My point is, you should physically appear the same in your photo(s) as you do in real life. I'm talking about looking *exactly* the same! We are not looking for modeling photos to show how great you can photograph. If your first name is "Ug" and your last name is "Lee," and you are "Ug Lee" fine, monster pictures are coming back—I'm sure you'll find work. Your photos should show who you are, even if you're so unattractive that you could be Freddy's nightmare.

There's acting work for your type. Whether you could make a good living doing scarecrow work; you've stuck your head out the window and gotten arrested for mooning; or, to be politically correct, you're anatomically compact, vertically-challenged, and folicly impaired; even if your ears can swat flies and you resemble Ross Perot, there is work for you.

If your photo doesn't accurately represent you, you'll be called in for roles that you are not right for. And, even worse, you won't be called in for parts you are right for. Misrepresenting yourself in your photos will waste your time and ours. There's a behind for every seat. Make sure your behind is sent in for the right parts, by resembling your photos.

Eventually, your photos will be sent to agents, casting directors and, ultimately, directors. If they like the physical "type" they see, they may call you in for an interview. A director receives your photo, in which you have blonde hair, a perfect nose, and an angelic face. The director loves the physical type he sees, so he calls you in for an interview.

But when you walk in the door you have dark hair, a nose that appears to be a third arm, and a face that would be less conspicuous in a zoo and that looks like a helicopter shot of Mt. St. Helens. Yes, everyone has a right to be ugly, but let's suppose you've abused the privilege. The director was looking for a specific type, and you've misrepresented yourself. You've wasted not only his time, but as importantly, yours.

You cut your own throat if the director was looking for someone with dark hair, a ski-nose, and a face that looks like a million—every year of it. He certainly wouldn't call you in, because in your photo you look beautiful and he was looking for someone who looks like a professional blind date. He really wanted someone who could look like a talent scout for a cemetery. Represent yourself accurately, because not everyone is beautiful. Let's just face it; most of us are barely presentable. "The camera takes a picture of what it sees." Bull! Make sure it sees you as you are, not as you'd like to be.

Don't confuse these photos with ones for the family album. If you need photos for Aunt Jenny and Uncle Jerry, fine. But keep them where they are supposed to be and don't use them as professional photos. Remember, you're only cutting your own throat if the photos don't accurately represent you.

Actors' regular "headshot" photos and publicity photos are two separate items. For casting purposes, actors use regular photos that shouldn't be confused with the publicity photos that stars use to sign autographs and for magazine articles. The latter are somewhat glamorized and not necessarily a very good representation of what the actor actually looks like. The bottom line is, your photo(s) should look just like you even if your doctor is a vet.

My computer notes with regards to photos show that the second most important point is that everyone seems to be looking for a certain trait. In auditions, the trait that comes up more times than any other is "personality." (This was covered in Chapter Seven.) How do you show that in your photos?

Finding the Right Photographer

You must find the right photographer. As you search for a photographer, keep the above things in mind. Splurge—go to a professional photographer who shoots actors for a living. I know actors don't like to spend a lot of money. Some actors wouldn't even buy a round of drinks at an Alcoholics Anonymous meeting and wouldn't even pick up the check at the Last Supper. However, obtaining good photos to promote your career is not the place to save money.

Check around to see what the price norm is in the particular city in which you plan to seek work as an actor. But be reasonable about it. If you can't decide whether to pay the photographer's fee or fly your family to Cairo, you're probably being overcharged. On the other hand, if it's between the photographer's fee and a down payment on a pair of socks, you're most likely being undercharged by someone who doesn't have a clue. Also, if the photographer shoots bar mitzvahs and weddings, I'd be careful. You don't want a jack-of-all trades.

Unless you only plan to work in a very small market, don't just go to any photographer who shoots glamour modeling shots. Acting photos should never look posed in any way whatsoever. Portrait photographers are not what you need here.

Although I said go to a photographer who shoots actors for a living, don't go to just anyone. Do your research. Use reliable sources of information on photographers, which are available in any city. The best source of information, of course, is from actors themselves. Word of mouth is always the best referral. Don't be afraid to ask around. A celebrity photo on a photographer's wall doesn't mean she actually shot that photo. Anyone can obtain photos of stars; they are sold all over the streets of Hollywood. Even if the photographer did take those celebrity photos, don't be impressed.

Names of good photographers can be obtained directly from agents' offices. Call a few agents' offices in the city in which you plan to work and ask the secretary which photographers they use for their clients. There's no need to bother the agent himself; the secretary should have all the information. But be careful. A few agents, even some semi-legitimate ones, will send you to a photographer who will kick back money to the agent. You want a photographer because an agent thinks he's the best, not because he's receiving money for the recommendation. Ask for agents to recommend three or four photographers, which lets you know there is probably no scheme here. Agents are some of the best sources for photographers, so don't hesitate to try and get recommendations from them.

If you're in New York or Los Angeles, look through the show-biz magazines *Backstage* or *Backstage West*, respectively, and you'll find many ads for photographers. This is kind of a last resort, because personal recommendations are preferable.

Before you decide on a particular photographer, ask to see some of her work. Base your decision on what she can do, and not on what she tells you. If she's a good photographer, she'll be more than happy to show you photos she's taken of other actors. Visit a few photographers before making a final decision.

Some of the things you want to inquire about are: Who keeps the negatives? (Photographers usually do, but it's better if you can.) How many rolls of film are going to be shot? How many 8 x 10s will you receive? How much will each additional 8 x 10 cost? Does the photographer have a hair and makeup person? Does that person cost extra or are the services included? If you don't like any of the photos, will she reshoot?

I can't stress enough how important it is to get fantastic photos of yourself, ones which show you as you really look. Pictures taken in high school for the yearbook, or photos that look like leftover mug shots from *60 Minutes*, simply won't do. There's no substitute for the best photos you can possibly obtain. You've come this far in your career. Spend a few extra bucks and go much further.

The Types of Photos You Will Need

At one time there was a huge distinction between theatrical (i.e., film and television) photos and commercial photos. That line is not so distinct anymore. It used to be that commercial photos were always full of huge smiles and theatrical photos were more dramatic. These days, to some extent, most actors use their commercial photo for some theatrical auditions and vice versa.

Basically, you can go three ways with your photos: You can obtain either a "headshot," a "three-quarter shot," or a "composite," depending on the medium you're after and the city in which you plan to work. Whatever the field, a headshot is essential. But many agents want a three-quarter shot and a headshot. The three-quarter shot has taken the place of the composite in Los Angeles and New York.

Like Jimmy Hoffa and Monty Python's parrot, composites in the major markets have ceased to exist. They are still used in the major markets for models and stuntmen, and in some of the smaller markets by a handful of actors. We'll mention composites here, but only in passing.

A headshot is just that—a shot of your head (i.e., face). There shouldn't be anyone else in the photo; that includes your pet! A typical headshot is taken from the middle of the bust line or the shoulders up. It should be printed on 8 x 10 paper. If you go into an agent's office with 5 x 7 photos or snapshots, you're displaying your naiveté about the professional world of acting.

The three-quarter shot is just that—a photo showing about three-quarters of your body, from about the knees up. Because it shows more of the body, having a headshot as well is a good idea. Many commercial casting directors like the three-quarter shot; about the same percentage only want a headshot. I strongly suggest that you have both. This way we see your face and get an idea of your entire look. (See examples of both the headshot and the three-quarter shot at the end of this chapter.)

A composite is just that—a composite of photos on an 8½ x 11 sheet of lithograph paper. It has a headshot on the front side and four or five photos on the back. Again, composites are rarely used these days.

Normally, the photos should be printed vertically and not horizontally. This may sound kind of ridiculous, but as we're sifting through the photos very quickly, we usually don't turn the horizontal ones. Some agents tell their actors to print their photos horizontally for the extra attention. Think twice before you do this. Since we rarely take the time to turn them around, we aren't likely to get a very good look at horizontal photos.

Some photographers are trying an interesting twist on this horizontal versus vertical discussion by putting a horizontal photo in a vertical format. In other words, the photo is printed across the paper horizontally, but the photo paper is still vertical. It is a concept worth considering. You should investigate all formats before making a final decision on how to print your photos.

Printing Your Name on the Photos

Since the photos will be presented to agents and casting directors with a resume attached to the back, having your name printed on the photo is optional. But it's highly recommended. Photos tend to become separated from their resumes in actual auditions. If your name is on the photo at least we'll have a reference. There are times actors don't get callbacks, or even jobs, because we can't find the photo to go with the right resume. Don't be like the actors who don't have their name or contact number on either their photo or their resume!

Your name should be printed at the bottom of the photo in such a way as to make it very visible. Printing it on a whited-out space, as opposed to printing it directly on the picture image, gives it more recognition. Names printed over the bottom part of the photo image are very hard to read. Don't forget that photos go by our faces very quickly. You might find it hard to believe, but directors are careful about what the screen background is when their name appears. A credit for the director's name in white on a cloudy, white background isn't going to stand out.

If you're going to put your name on the image, and the image is dark at the bottom, have the type reversed out in white lettering to make it stand out. (The opposite is also true.) Just be sure to contrast your name and its background. Some actors, once they obtain an agent, like to have their agent's name printed on the bottom of the headshot on the opposite side of their name.

Unless you are "Cher," don't use just one name. Print your first and last name. Since many models use one name on their "zed cards," which are not used by actors, when someone only lists one name we immediately think that person is a model. Directors have a bad joke that says, "The reason he only printed one name is because he's a model and models are too stupid to know their last name." Obviously models aren't stupid by any stretch of the imagination and I find this kind of saying offensive, but it exists, so take it for what it's worth and don't print only one name on your photos. Some actors also use their middle name. Although there are exceptions, it's usually not a good idea because it causes confusion.

Popular belief has it that no two members of SAG can use the same name professionally. But in reality SAG cannot deny a member the use of a professional name if it's the member's legal name. It is *highly recommended* that you do not use the exact same name as another actor. SAG discourages this use, and for good reasons! If you have the same legal name as another actor and you insist on using that name, SAG will have you sign a form stating that they are not liable for any mix-ups of any kind, such as residual checks, etc.

I suggest that before you print your name on your photos, check with the union(s) to see if anyone is currently using the same name. Even if you do check and you're not already a member, and you find no one is presently using your name, by the time you join the union(s) they might be. At least you're doing everything you can in advance to try to preserve your name. You're going to be working very hard to get people to remember your name, after all. Why get your name out there only to give publicity to another actor!

Meeting the Photographer

Whichever way you go with your photos, be it a headshot, a three-quarter shot, or the rarely-used composite, there are a few basic things to keep in mind once you have chosen a photographer.

Before the shooting, make an appointment with your photographer to discuss makeup, clothing, backgrounds, and other particulars. Decide these things beforehand so that the shooting can go smoothly. If you spend most of the scheduled time discussing the particulars that should have been worked out in advance, you waste the photographer's time and your money. You have lost more "shooting time" with the photographer.

When to Shoot Your Photos

A great time to shoot your photos is at "magic hour." Directors and cinematographers use this term to designate the time right after sunrise and right before sunset. The lighting on your face is perfect at this time of day. Shadows aren't harsh. The light is very even across the face and has a "magic" glow to it. In fact, many times directors will only shoot special scenes at "magic hour."

If I was directing an automobile commercial and wanted the car to have a "magic" look to it, I'd want to shoot it at this time. Because "magic hour" limits "shooting time," it might take four or five days to get that perfect thirty-second commercial shot.

If the photographer wants to shoot your photos at high noon, I'd try to change her mind, or think twice about using that particular photographer. Insist on the time of day that you prefer. No photographer can make a living just shooting actors at the best time of day, so he'll try to get other actors to choose different times. Time of day is relevant, of course, only if you are shooting outdoors.

Whether to shoot your photos indoors or outdoors will depend upon many factors; time of day, season, your agent's (if you have one) personal preference, what the norm is in the city in which you plan to work, and so on.

Color or Black-and-White?

It used to be that actors' photos were almost always back-and-white. The reasons are mostly a matter of cost. With the advent of new technology, color is relatively inexpensive. Back-and-white photos are still in the majority, but color photos are coming into their own. If you don't have an agent, whether to use color or black-and-white is a personal preference. If you do have an agent, then this should be a decision made jointly by you and your agent.

Actors with red hair should *definitely* consider using color in their photos. Red hair is a real commodity. From a directing standpoint, having a variety of hair-colors on the screen is a plus. There are, of course, many blondes and brunettes to choose from, but fewer redheads.

Out-of-Date Photos

All your photos should be up-to-date. You don't want a picture that was done by Leonardo da Vinci. You probably no longer resemble the person in your high school photos; all those freckles and your acne are gone. An old photo taken at Disneyland with Donald Duck is cute, but not very professional. Don't laugh. I receive such photos on a daily basis.

Update your photos at least every two years, preferably every year. If you're a senior citizen, then perhaps you could wait longer. A year won't matter as much to a seventy-two-year-old as it does to an eight-year-old. Young performers, especially, should have their photos updated annually since they change so often.

Stage photos could possibly be shot every two to three years. But for screen acting, which is up-close, and the audience is right in your face, photos need to be updated more frequently.

Of course, anytime you change your appearance, your photos should be redone. If an actor was sporting a beard the last time he was photographed but has now shaved it, he'll need new photos. If a woman cuts her hair drastically, new photo time! An alert to actors who have beards and mustaches that make it appear as though they have to be grounded during hunting season: These appendages rarely work commercially.

Personality in Photos

Your commercial photos should be very "alive"; they should have a very "up" feeling. For a theatrical headshot, smiles can also be a plus, if that's the type of characters you're most likely going to play. Still, if you're the warm, friendly type, your photos shouldn't make it appear as though you could make a laughing hyena get depressed. Smiling is the cheapest way to improve your looks. Especially for a commercial photo, you should show your pearly-whites, even if you have a heart of gold and teeth to match. After looking at a group of photos I'm always thinking I could perhaps get the Kevorkian group rate, since everyone looks so mean. You know on the Wild World of Sports where that guy goes flying down the ski-slope and the announcer says, ". . . and the agony of defeat"? Don't appear as though you pushed him.

This isn't to say you can't have a very serious or mean looking shot in addition to a smiling one. In fact, it is recommended that for theatrical headshots, you have a serious shot also. But, the main theatrical headshot should just be a "you" shot.

By bringing a few different headshots into the audition, you're giving us a choice of which headshot(s) is more appropriate for the role we happen to be casting at that moment. I know casting directors who don't like to have to choose from a wide variety of photos. They want you to choose. I don't think bringing in two shots is excessive and will tax anyone's brain too much.

Should You Use Makeup?

Some makeup is appropriate. But the photos shouldn't be taken with gobs of makeup on your face so that it looks as if it was put on with a paint roller. Makeup that is applied with a putty knife, has to be removed with a chisel, needs an estimate, requires scaffolding and an environmental impact study will only demonstrate how little you know about the acting profession. Keep in mind, photos accentuate makeup, making it look thicker than it actually is. You shouldn't look like Petey from the *Little Rascals*.

As with choosing a photographer, don't just get any makeup artist; find someone who knows what type of makeup you need for the particular field of acting that you're interested in pursuing. Photographers who specialize in shooting actors' photos can often give you information on makeup artists.

You probably already know that makeup for your photos is extremely different from street makeup. It should be very subtle so that you don't appear phony. Basically, men shouldn't wear any makeup unless they have shine on their forehead and need powder.

For commercial photos, makeup should be even more subtle than that used for TV and film photos. In your photos, you don't want to look like an "actor." "Everyday looking people" work much more frequently than do the model types, because of more public identity. If you are a gorgeous model type, then your photos should represent you as such, but keep the above in mind.

Stage actors on stage use much thicker makeup than that used for TV and films because, obviously, the audience is at a further distance. More lines are used under the eyes, down the nose, and so on, because otherwise the face becomes "lost" in the distance. Your photos used for stage, as far as makeup is concerned, should be somewhat like the ones used for TV and film. In other words, the less makeup the better. Your challenge is to find a makeup person who knows the difference.

Should You Retouch Your Photos?

Retouching a photo is fine; spray painting is not! As a general rule, it's okay to retouch anything that isn't permanently on your face. If you have a blemish on your face, for example, that will evaporate by the time the photo is developed, then by all means manipulate it in Adobe Photoshop. But if something is on your face that's not going away soon, then don't airbrush it out. For instance, if you have so many pimples that a blind man can read your face, it's best not to retouch the photos.

Photo Wardrobe

Choose clothes for your photo shoot carefully. They should be "appropriate" and not very sexy, unless these are the types of parts for which you'll primarily be reading. Make sure they are clean, but they needn't be fancy. They should convey a down-to-earth, everyday-life feeling. Don't get carried away; you don't want such down-to-earth clothes that it looks as though you get your fashion tips from Anna Nicole Smith.

Be careful about wearing anything with writing on it. After seeing hundreds of actors we become tired and bored in auditions and we will try to read what's written on shirts. Have you ever found yourself at a party talking to someone who has writing on his shirt? Your eyes keep drifting down to the writing to try to read it, and you're distracted.

Patterns on shirts and blouses can be distracting. Designs on tops with little lines running vertically or horizontally, or those with little patterns that bleed together are also distracting. I mentioned that you shouldn't wear floral or paisley shirts in an audition. The same applies for your photos. Generally, solids are better than patterned tops, since you don't want to wear anything that is louder than a Christmas tie.

If they aren't too busy, sometimes plaid shirts can work well for commercial auditions, but they don't always work as well for commercial photos, since they can distract from your face. Subtle plaids are very neutral both for auditions and photos; they don't come in or go out of style. We have a saying in the entertainment business: "It won't play in Iowa," or "They'll love it in Iowa." Iowa is considered the most average state in the U.S. We love for our shows and commercials to do well in Iowa because if they do, they will probably play well nationally.

Why do you think the candidates scramble to make Iowa one of their first stops when a presidential election is coming up? They know that it's important to sell to the heartland. Guess what? A lot of people in Iowa wear plaid. I'll repeat: Although plaids work well in commercial auditions, they may be too busy for your headshot(s). With regards to photos, solids generally work best.

As a rule, black-and-white shirts, especially in a black-and-white photo, aren't desirable. You should wear a shirt that makes your face stand out; one whose color contrasts well with your skin color will most effectively do this. Of course, in a black-and-white photo it is the shade and not necessarily the color that will either make your face stand out or blend it into the background.

Revealing Your Face

For your photos, don't cover your face with anything whatsoever—sunglasses, hands, shadows, hats, etc. When we are viewing photos, we're not looking for a reason to call you into an audition; we're looking for a reason *not* to call you in. We have too many photos from which to choose. If an actor is covering, or partially covering his face with long hair down the front (i.e., "Cousin It"), I'm going to hear from the client something to the effect of, "He's covering a shrapnel wound. Let's move on."

Avoid turtlenecks and sweaters with high necklines. Whenever you cover your neck we assume that you have something to hide. You're not selling clothes with these photos; you're selling "you." In order to eliminate as many actors as possible, we will look for any excuse whatsoever to discard a photo. Don't give us more reasons by covering up your face or neck.

What About Glasses?

If you wear glasses, no problem. Just take some photos with the glasses on and some without. I suggest "non-glare" glasses, but check with your eye-care professional first. Wearing non-glare glasses is important in the photo and more important on an actual audition. If you do need the glasses to read for an audition, then slate (covered in further detail in Chapter Fifteen) with them off and put them on for the actual audition. Then everyone can see two different "yous."

As a tip, even if you don't need glasses you might want to get some that have regular glass in them. Then you can slate with them on and take them off for the actual reading. I can't tell you how many times I'll phone the casting director and ask to see a particular actor again, but without the glasses or vice versa. We may like one look over the other.

Photo Backgrounds

Your photographer and you should choose your backgrounds. There should be no distracting objects in the photo. I once saw a headshot where the actor was standing up against a house. There was a potted plant in the window behind him. But you couldn't see the pot because his head was in the way. So, you have this tree growing out of the top of this guy's head. It was funny and we all laughed. After he left, none of us could recall his face.

Another headshot that comes to mind had been taken in the actor's agent's office. You know those clocks that many modeling agencies have in the lobby that tell you what time it is in London, Rome, and who knows where else? (Like we care.) The actor was standing up against the wall (a bad background) and you could see a huge clock on either side of the actor's head. The clocks looked like two huge ears. We all broke out into a rendition of "M-I-C-K-E-Y, M-O-U-S-E" and had a good laugh. But, again, none of us could remember what his face looked like at the end of the day.

Phony indoor backdrops with scenes painted on them are a definite no-no; take photos with natural backgrounds. Natural backgrounds make the actor look, well, more "natural." A good example would be a park with out-of-focus trees in the background. Objects at different lengths from the lens give depth to the photo, which will make the face of the actor "come off" the page. Although the photo is actually 2-D, it should appear 3-D.

Where to Focus Your Eyes

While being photographed look directly into the lens. Don't look to the right or to the left. It's a psychological advantage to look right into the lens. There's something that makes a director feel guilty about throwing your headshot away when you're looking right into the camera. If you have children you know how hard it is to say "no" to them when they look you right in the eyes. When you look right into the lens, you are looking the person who is viewing the photo right in the eyes.

Don't squint like Mr. Eastwood. It works for him, but probably won't for you. Remember, we're looking for a reason to toss your headshot into the trash. When a shot shows an actor squinting in a photo, someone is bound to say, "She has light-sensitive eyes. Next." Sound kind of stupid? Yes, but we don't need much of a reason to toss your headshot.

Hiding Weight (or Anything Else)

Hiding weight in your photos is a no-no. Guys, if you have a Liquid Grain Storage Facility (beer gut) and had to be baptized at Sea

World, fine. We may be looking for such a type. But if we're not looking for that type and we call you into an audition because we don't see that in your photo, you'll have been called in for a part for which you're not right. As I stated earlier, represent yourself accurately.

What About Borders?

Borders—should you, or shouldn't you? You'll probably get as many answers on this one as there are people in the industry. My personal opinion is, a border is helpful. It forces the viewer's eyes right toward the center of the photograph, which is probably going to be your face. Photos that bleed to the edges, usually don't force the eye inward. This is my personal preference. Either way is acceptable.

Product Names

Take care not to show product names in your photos. If you're drinking a can of 7-Up in one of your photos and you go on an audition for a Coke commercial, there is an obvious conflict of interest. It might not prevent you from being called back on the Coke commercial, but it is safer not to show any product names. This rule applies to commercial photos especially, but I would be careful about showing product names on any of your photos. It could be that Burger King is sponsoring that movie-of-the-week you're auditioning for wearing a McDonalds t-shirt.

What Separates a Good Photo From a Bad One?

When it comes to selecting your photos, let the photographer help you pick them, but don't just go by her recommendations. If you have an agent, then allow the agent to pick the final photos to be used. After all, that agent is in the marketplace day after day and knows what's selling and what isn't better than anyone. Aunt Fanny and Uncle Bob shouldn't have a voice here. What looks great on the living-room piano has nothing to do with what sells in the marketplace.

One way to tell a good photo from a bad one is to stare straight ahead. Hold your photo at eye level to your left. Do not move your eyes to the left or right. Then pass the photo by your face to the right fairly quickly. That's how fast it goes by our faces. On that pass, if anything stands out more than your face—hair, background, clothes, etc., then you might want to consider a new headshot, because the face is the most important thing in your headshot.

Normally, I don't think that because someone is a friend he should have any voice in what photos you use, but here's an exception. It's another way to gauge whether your photos are marketable. Take your theatrical headshot to ten of your friends. Ask them, "What types of roles do you see me playing with this photo?"

If they can name many types of roles they see you playing, then that's a good headshot. If they say, "I see you playing a professor, a pastor, a pervert, a president,"—not that those are mutually exclusive—then they have named many characters. If they are hemming and hawing around, "Gosh, let's see here, I don't really know . . . . maybe a sperm donor," then they don't "see" enough characters in your photos.

Try the same with your commercial photo. Ask, "What types of products do you see me selling when you look at this photo?" If your friends see you representing many products—Burger King, Coke, Crest toothpaste, Ford automobiles, for example, then that would be a good commercial photo. Should they be able to name only one type of product—"Perhaps, a cotton stuffer for aspirin bottles," then your photo is too limiting.

Friends and family, unless they happen to be in the business, are the worst people you could use to help you choose photos. The previous example is just one way of establishing how sellable your photos actually are.

Reproducing Your Photos

Once your photo(s) are taken and you have decided which one(s) you want to use for your headshot and/or three-quarter shot, have them duplicated. Save the contact sheets, or "proof sheets" as they are commonly referred to in the acting business; they can be helpful when you're being interviewed by an agent. (We'll discuss this in Chapter Twelve.)

Go to a special photography store that mass-duplicates photos. In the larger cities certain photo labs cater to actors. Find out about such services from other actors, your photographer, and agents. *The Yellow Pages* generally isn't a good place to look. As when searching for good photographers, referrals are always preferred.

Reproduced copies will never look as good as your original. Therefore, it is imperative that you see a "proof" of the reproduced version first. This allows you to decide on the tone and shades of the reproduced copies. Otherwise, you're leaving this very important decision up to whoever happens to be duplicating your photos that day.

Choose either glossy, matte, or pearl finishes on your photos. These finishes give the photo depth, which tends to make your face stand out more. Lithographs are cheaper, but they tend to "flatten" the photo.

To get started in the major markets, you'll need between two hundred and three hundred of these photos. So now that you have marvelous photographs of yourself, do you take several copies of them and start knocking on directors' and casting directors' doors? No. You simply must have an agent. But before you go looking for an agent, you'll need a resume to go along with your headshot, which will be discussed in the next chapter.

Kevin Cater

Photo by Schultz Bros. Photography

Sample Headshot

Photo by Schultz Bros. Photography

Cheyenne Overall

Sample Headshot

Photo by Schultz Bros. Photography

Charlie Scola

Sample Three-Quarter Shot

CHAPTER TEN

Do Compose a Good Resume

So you worked at McDonald's for four years in a row and are thinking how wonderful this experience will look on your resume. Or you were a foreman at your hometown Ford plant, and executives there told you to use them as a reference. No! No! These types of references will be of no help whatsoever on your acting resume. Directors won't be hiring you for anything except acting, and we don't care what your previous employers think of you. Directors care what *they* think of you and what you think of *yourself.*

You say that in your play productions you worked the light-board and the sound equipment, and took tickets at the theater door. You were probably told how important it is to learn all aspects of the theater. I perfectly agree. It is important for an actor to know what is going on around him.

If you intend to be an actor, however, your resume should mostly contain information with regards to your acting experience. You probably won't ever see the light-board or understand the sound equipment, and no director is going to hire you to take tickets at the door. In fact, when you're hired as a screen actor, if you lift a prop, touch a light, or do anything with any equipment, all of which are under the purview of theatrical unions, and you aren't a member of that union, the union could file a grievance against you. According to the unions, you are taking someone else's job away from him. Directors care about what you, an actor, can do in *front* of the camera and *on* stage, not behind them.

"I don't have any acting credits," you say. Haven't you already been through your initial training period? My remarks are based on that assumption. If not, start acting in plays and taking acting classes! Without acting credits, your professional acting resume will basically be a blank sheet, except for a few other important items that should be listed, and which I will discuss later in this chapter.

The Purpose of the Resume (to a Director)

What's the real purpose of the resume? Like the photo, the purpose of an actor's resume differs for a director than for an agent or casting director. The latter two want to see what you've been in and what your experiences have been. And to some extent this is true for the director. But in addition to seeing what you've been in, directors might possibly want to view your work.

It happens many times that I've requested a copy of a film to view a certain actor's work, only to find out that he didn't appear in the film. What if you were in a film, but were eventually cut out? We do a lot of editing. (Someday you'll see *The Five Commandments* on TV.) This happens and is mostly no fault of the actor. Directors can phone the production company, the Screen Actors Guild, or visit the IMDB website to verify if you were in the film and then cut. We understand. But we don't understand actors who outright lie to us.

So don't lie about any credits! Your resume shouldn't win a Pulitzer Prize for fiction. The credibility of your resume shouldn't have stretch marks. One way or another you'll get caught. We don't trust liars. For the kind of money we spend on productions, we need people we can trust. Yes, actors on TV talk shows do mention how they lied on their resumes when they first got into this business.

You are hearing about a few who were lucky and didn't get caught. What you don't hear about are the thousands of actors who get caught every day, most of whom don't even know that we caught them! In the old days, we didn't have the Internet. Now there is so much more information available to us at our fingertips that we didn't have years ago.

Your resume should be one page only. Cut out the fat; don't make your resume look as though it has been "padded." The resume samples included in this chapter do not have to be followed in any one exact form or wording, but do be consistent in form and clear in presentation.

This probably goes without saying, but I'm saying it anyway: Don't use cheap paper. The difference in cost between using good paper and cheap paper is so little that it's not worth saving a few pennies.

Many new actors use the normal business resume format for their acting resume, but there are major differences between the two, which I'll outline. We don't care about your objectives and career goals. We already know those by the fact that you want an acting career. The format I illustrate is very standard in the industry, although some parts of the country may have slight variations.

Contact Information

At the top center of the page type your name. In the right-hand corner, but spaced down below your name, list your agent (if you have one) and her address and phone number. If you don't have an agent, then you'll list some personal contact number. A cell phone is great; if not, a beeper and/or answering machine number will do. If an agent, or anyone in this business for that matter, can't get in touch with you or leave a message on the first try, few will continue phoning.

If you plan to work in Los Angeles, no matter where you actually live, try to have a Los Angeles or surrounding area address. The same is true for New York City. Maybe you have a friend who will let you use his address. Or get a P.O. box. And the same rule applies to having a local phone number. Agents, and others, don't want to be responsible for you leaving your family and moving out to Los Angeles. If nothing happens with your career, then with most agents there is the guilt factor.

Once you have an agent, never list your personal contact number on your resume again; list your agent's name (or agency), address, and phone number. Your agent will be sending your photos and resumes all over the city (perhaps all over the country), and you'll have no idea who will see them. You don't want some big-city pervert phoning you at home. Let him phone your agent, and your agent can deal with him—that's part of the agent's job.

You can also list your e-mail address and website address in the same corner, if you have them. A website is the perfect place for someone wanting to find out more about you. I do have to admit that very few people in the industry have the time to visit actors' websites, but list yours anyway.

Listing of Unions

Below your name you'll want to list any acting unions of which you are a member. If you're a member of the Screen Actors Guild (SAG), the American Federation of Television and Radio Artists (AFTRA), or Actors Equity Association (known as "Equity" or AEA), you'll want to mention this. (These unions, and related ones, will be discussed in detail in Chapter Eleven.) On a resume always abbreviate the union affiliations—SAG, AFTRA, Equity, etc.

If you have fulfilled the eligibility requirements for joining SAG but haven't joined yet, it is absolutely correct to list "SAG eligible." Although this isn't always the case, it informs directors that you have probably been on a SAG set and have some knowledge of what takes place there.

Your Age

Below your name you'll list some important items. Some actors in smaller cities list their "Age Range," as an indication of the range of ages they can possibly play. It doesn't matter how old you actually are so long as you are not a minor. The crucial matter is how old or young you appear to be.

If you list "Age Range," the younger you are, the narrower it will be. Examples of age ranges could be 7-10, 15-20, 30-40, 60-75. These are only examples and your age range could fall anywhere in between these numbers. Few people can play 15-40; in fact,, none on film without greatly altering their natural look.

I very strongly believe it is always a major mistake for an actor to list his "Age Range," no matter in which city you are working. I mean, *always* a major mistake. Take what I am saying very seriously, because I don't use the word "always" very often. I agree with the agents and casting directors who feel that listing your age range puts you into a category that limits your selling ability. And, unless you are under the age of eighteen, certainly never list your actual age. Even then, you would just list your birth date. We need this information if you are a minor because of the child labor laws.

Whatever you do, don't represent yourself as being over eighteen if you are not. We'll find out anyway when you start working for us. If you're dishonest about being a minor, you could mess up an entire shooting schedule on a TV show, film, or commercial.

As a director, I have very strict legal guidelines on the number of hours a day I can work minors. So it's a real advantage for actors to be over eighteen years old, but to appear younger. When we're casting someone who is supposed to be sixteen or seventeen, we'll look very hard to find an actor who is actually eighteen years of age or older.

One time I was auditioning women for a commercial. We were looking for someone 20 to 23 years of age. After seeing actors for a week or so, I was getting pretty discouraged since the right person hadn't come in the door. Finally, an actor named Sharon arrived; she gave a great reading and was perfect for the part. She was extremely attractive—I've never seen skin so well organized.

Against Screen Actors Guild rules, the client asked her actual age. People asking you this question may not be aware of the rule. If you are asked, give them an age range that you can play, making sure the range is within the one which they are looking for the role! Again, the only exception to this rule is if someone is under the age of eighteen. (I know I advised against putting an age range on a resume, but if you're outright asked your age, then verbally tell them your age range.)

Sharon told us she was twenty-eight. After she left the audition, the client turned to me and said that Sharon was perfect for the part, but a little too old. More weeks passed and I really wanted Sharon for the part, so I came up with a plan. I phoned her and asked her to come back to the audition. I asked her, since the client insisted on asking the actors their age, would she please tell him she was twenty-three-years-old?

No, one shouldn't lie. But, the client shouldn't have been asking her for her actual age either. This is the only place I say that an actor should be somewhat creative about the truth. If they ask you to give an age and you know the age range of the character they are looking for, then give an age range in that range. Otherwise, never, ever be dishonest.

Sharon was a little nervous about this, thinking that the client would remember her age. I informed her that after seeing that many actors he wouldn't remember her age; in fact, he wouldn't even remember her!

She came back to the audition, and sure enough this client asked Sharon her age. She said she was twenty-three. He told her she was perfect for the part and would hear from us. After she walked out the door, he wanted to stop the auditions because he was so happy with Sharon. You guessed it! We hired Sharon. Be very careful about age. People get an image of you based on it.

If you're so old that you wrote the foreword to the Bible, so much the better. There is work for every age group. Yes, it's true that there is more work for teenagers and very young adults, but there are also a huge number of actors in that age range trying to obtain those same roles.

Height, Weight, Eyes, Hair

Next list your height and weight. If you're eight feet tall and so big you can only play seek, or so short you can play handball up against the curb, then represent yourself as such; so much the better. All types are needed for TV, film, commercials, and stage. Anything that makes you stand out from the rest of the crowd will someday be a plus.

Don't lie about your height or weight. We don't care if you weigh anything from "Why don't they tie me up and force-feed me a Twinkie?" to your yearbook picture continues on the next page and you can legally apply for group insurance. Whatever! We just want you to be honest so that we'll call you in for parts you're right for.

Consider an interesting point: TV and film add about ten pounds to your appearance. The screen actually stretches you out. Movies in the theaters are even worse, because they stretch more from side to side than they do from top to bottom. In other words, the image is more of a rectangle. It stretches you more horizontally. Directors are very aware of the appearance of extra poundage. However, don't add that extra weight beforehand to this statistic on your resume.

Next you'll list eyes and hair. For stage resumes this category is less important than for screen resumes, but I think it's generally a good idea to list this information on any acting resume, especially one used for commercials. If you have different shades of color for your hair, fine, then have different resumes with the different colors on them.

With multiple resumes, bring the appropriate resume that fits the hair color you happen to have that day, when you come in to audition. The bottom line is, we don't care if your hair is our favorite shade of peroxide, or if you're a cross between a brunette and a drugstore. Perhaps your hair has more extensions than AT&T. Whatever the case, accurately represent yourself visually on your resume so that later we can match you visually with your resume and headshot. Those of you who have a toupee, please have a great one. Spend the extra money and get a "piece" that looks incredibly real. Don't skimp (pardon the pun) on this one. In a close-up, the audience will see each strand of hair!

No other statistics should be listed. Models put their bust, shoe and dress size, etc. Actors don't need to list these. There's nothing wrong with being a model, but for some weird reason many directors think if you're a model you can't act. It's not fair and it usually isn't true, but this isn't a fair business.

If a potential employer needs this extra statistical information he can contact your agent to obtain it. And that would be a good thing, because then your agent can "sell" you over the phone.

For your credits sections, you'll work in three columns, which are easy to read.

Film Credits

For a TV, film, and commercial resume, you'll next want to list any film credits you might have in a left-hand column. This includes anything shot on film—feature film, educational film, corporate film, industrial film, student film, etc. If the project was shot on film, but is only being shown on television, then put it in the subheading, Television, which will be discussed next. In a center column record the "billing" that precedes your name—Star, Guest Star, Co-Star, Featuring, Introducing, etc. If you have no billing but you did speak dialogue, you should list "Principal." With nothing listed, it will be assumed that you were an extra.

Billing is negotiable and doesn't necessarily bear any relation to the size of the part. In fact, billing can be one of the stickiest negotiation points. Many things go along with negotiating an actor's billing, such as the placement. It is very important whether an actor's billing appears "above the title," on the main titles, or on the end title crawl. The size of the letters—height and boldness—is negotiable, as is the length of time the actor's name will appear on screen. Will a number of other names appear on the screen at the same time, called "shared card," or will the actor's name appears by itself, called "single card"? Will the word "and" be inserted before the actor's name, separating it from the rest of the names? What about an "and" and an "as" before your name? Maybe your agent wants "and Jim Clark as Tommy Owens" in the main title lineup.

Everyone in the industry is very particular about how their billing will be presented. One of the feature films I directed at a major studio had an Academy Award-winning actor in it. On all of the posters and other advertising, the studio's art department forgot to put a box around the actor's name. This omission obliged the studio to recall every poster and bit of advertising and redo them with the actor's name inside a box. Was the actor justified in having everything redone? Absolutely! I backed him 100 percent. It was part of his negotiated deal and he deserved to have it. By the way, the studio had no problem redoing all of the advertising.

At times actors aren't offered much money for a role, but in exchange are offered higher billing than the part deserves. Take the higher billing! It looks great on a resume. We realize that higher billing doesn't necessarily mean a larger role, but it still impresses us!

Don't list the name of the character you portrayed. If you believe I am incorrect, look at it this way: Think of the last film you viewed. Do you remember the character names or the actor's names? I bet you're hard-pressed to name two or three of the characters' names. Can you name one? Aren't the few characters you do name likely to be ones of the starring actors?

If for some reason people would be able to identify a character name of yours, then list it, but this would be a very rare occasion. An example might be if you were a regular on a very popular TV series, or a very memorable character in a top grossing film. Even then, it would probably be better to list your billing.

If you insist on listing the character you played, then just list the name, but don't write out "Played the part of...." Directors don't read sentences on resumes. We're seeing a lot of actors on an audition and don't have time to read sentences. We like to glance very quickly at the resume and see things in neat columns.

The third column should state the name of the production company that shot the film, which is important because it not only gives credibility to your resume, it also informs directors where they can obtain a copy of the project.

Television Credits

List any television credits you might have next. Use the same three-column format as you did for film credits. In the first, list the name of the show; in the second, the billing; and in the third, the production company that produced it or the network on which it aired.

Any film, tape, or DVD of yourself that you have available—be it TV, feature film, student film, etc.—should be mentioned prominently as "Tape Available," "Film Available," "DVD Available," etc. (depending on which format it happens to be). Even though your scenes should be transferred to videotape or DVD if they're on film, the actor's industry jargon tends to refer to this as having "film on yourself." (Student films, "film on yourself," and preparing your demo reel for agents are all covered in Chapter Eleven.)

Most cities have local cable access stations. Contact them to see if you can be on one of their shows. Perhaps you could do a monologue or two-person scene while they record you. Although this is not ideal footage on you, if it looks professional it might be of some help. Just make sure that it doesn't look "local," because your competition will have footage from actual well-known TV shows and films. In some cases, "film" of this type might be okay to show to an agent, but isn't really what you want to show to a casting director or director.

Commercials

The next category is "Commercials." In most of the major markets I highly recommend that you do *not* list the actual commercials you've been in, even though in some of the smaller markets many agents will want you to list them, by product name.

I can think of many times in auditions when we didn't call a particular actor in because he had a competing product listed on his resume. It's natural that you want to list that huge national commercial you were in, but one of the purposes of the resume is to help you obtain work. Anytime your resume inhibits you from obtaining work the resume has totally defeated one of its main purposes.

You can't shoot commercials for competing products until you have been let go from the original product. Don't even try! You'll get caught and you will end up in a lawsuit from the original company that made the first product. You can count on that!

In the major markets your resume should just state "List Available Upon Request," under the "Commercials" heading, even if your list consists of only one commercial. Usually no one except agents, who are just curious, will even ask what commercials you've been in, but if they do, be honest. Truth to tell, I don't know of any actors who actually have a list preprinted.

I'm aware that some actors list "Conflicts Upon Request," under Commercials. I would steer clear of this wording. Why remind everyone that you have "conflicts"? Yes, we know that you probably do, but why emphasize it?

Stage Roles

Following "Commercials" is the "Stage Roles" category. (Note: A stage resume should list "Stage Roles" before it lists "Film" and "Television" credits.) For a stage resume, stage credits are very important for obvious reasons. They are also important to TV sitcom and soap opera directors and casting directors because both of these formats are shot somewhat like a stage play. And film directors like them because it shows that you are actively honing your skills as an actor.

The first column will list the name of the play. The second column names the character you actually played. (This differs from film and television roles, because we know character names from stage plays much better than we do for TV and film characters.) The third column lists the theater name and the city in which it is located. When the theater name contains the name of the city (e.g., Burbank Little Theatre, Denver Center Theatre), then the city need not be listed separately.

Broadway and Off-Broadway credits should be listed in a separate category to make them stand out. Use three columns to list the show, the role you played, and the name of the theater in which you performed.

Stage credits don't carry as much weight on a screen resume as TV and film acting credits. But, if you don't have any TV or film credits, then stage credits take on more importance.

No matter what professional medium the resume is being used for, school and community plays carry very little weight on your *professional* acting resume. You must realize that when you auditioned for those local plays you were auditioning up against other people from local areas. Now you're in a whole new ball game—you're no longer up against locals, but against stars with household names, whose TV series were just canceled and they need the work, also. But, if you don't have many professional acting credits, then you should list any college dramatic productions or community theater plays in which you performed.

Listing high school play credits is a controversial topic. I would say that if you're still in high school, then maybe, and that's only a "maybe," you should list those high school credits. If you're going to list them, do it in such a way that it doesn't appear to be a school in the first place. For example, you performed some plays at John Anderson High School; then you could list it as "John Anderson Auditorium," or "John Anderson Theatre" in the third column. That's not lying; the school does have an auditorium or theater even if it's a cafeteria converted for the evening.

The alternative would be to list the name of the drama organization that put on, or is responsible for, the play. At the high school mentioned above you might have the "John Anderson Players," or whatever. Most directors would assume that these were done at some community theater and community theater plays have more weight than high school plays. You could list college productions, which are much more acceptable on a professional resume than are high school credits.

What if you don't have any, or very few, stage credits? Some acting teachers and even some agents will tell you to list a play and the corresponding character that you performed in an acting class to make it appear as though you were in the actual play. I strongly recommend that you don't use this practice. Honesty is the best policy. But, if you must use this practice, be sure you have at least read the play and are very familiar with it. When I was an actor back when bacon, eggs, milk and sunshine were good for you, I appeared in several Broadway plays. When an actor comes in and has one of those productions on his resume, I naturally like to talk about that show. Many times they have had no idea what the plot of the play was.

These days actors usually do list "understudy" roles. Deciding whether to list understudy roles should be based on their status and on the number of other credits you might have. If you were understudying a name actor in a name show, this would carry a lot of weight.

In this case, after the name of the character you played, write "(Understudy)," or "(u/s)." If you have numerous understudy roles, and very few regular ones, you might want to list the understudy roles in a separate category heading, "Understudy Roles," or "U/S" following the category of "Stage Roles" and before the next category.

Be careful about listing a whole lot of theater credits on a screen resume if you have no TV and film credits. It is unfair, but many screen directors will assume you'll overact. To deal with this, many actors put the words "Representative Roles" in parentheses right beside the words "Stage Roles." They list their most important credits and some that "represent" the types of roles they have played. By doing this, it shortens your list and makes you appear less of a stage actor and more of a screen actor. This doesn't mean you should stop performing in plays. Absolutely not! Keep honing your craft.

Multiple theater credits from the same theater or organizations are a positive. It shows that you probably got along personally with people at the theater and that they wanted to work with you again. That might be somewhat of a stretch, but we try to extract whatever information we can from your resume.

Theatrical Training

The next category to list is "Theatrical Training," which includes vocal training and/or dance training; in other words, any performance-related training should be listed here. Training is becoming more and more important. Budgets are climbing higher each year and we seem to be taking less chances these days on people who aren't well trained. Your training, or lack thereof, gives us a good indication of how serious you are about this business.

High school drama courses shouldn't be listed; no one in the professional acting arena cares. As with play production credits, college training is okay to list, but professional acting workshops are preferable.

I believe universities and colleges are great places to get training because you can learn your craft there, at least for theater. You can't learn your craft on network television or on an actual feature film. By the time you get to these arenas you had better already know your craft. Some universities have a fine faculty and some of the nicest theaters with the best equipment are found there. There's too much "academia" on the minds of some university professors. Many of them have B.A.'s, M.A.'s, and Ph.D's, but few have J.O.B.'s. Some have a PBS mind in an MTV world. This is somewhat tongue-in-cheek, but check out what professional experience your college professor has had in the real world. You might be pleasantly surprised or horribly disappointed. Either way, university theater can be a very good training ground for actors.

Again, it's easier for us to read your resume if you keep everything in neat columns. List the name of the class in the first column, the instructor in the middle column, and the organization sponsoring the class or the name of the school where it was held in the third column. If you have a college degree in acting, you don't need to list all of the classes you took. Just listing the degree will suffice.

Special Abilities

Lastly, list any "Special Abilities" you have. This category is more important for a screen resume than for a stage one; you'll be performing more activities on the screen than on stage. (Exception: Singing and dancing abilities are extremely important on a stage resume.) You should list such abilities as snow-skiing, rollerblading, skateboarding, horseback riding, musical instruments that you play, motorcycle riding, singing and dancing, accents and dialects you can use, and so on.

Make sure you list "accents" and "dialects" correctly. Do you know the difference between the two? Assuming you're in the United States, people who come from the southern part of the country do not have a Southern accent. There's no such thing as a Southern accent here. By definition, "accents" are foreign and "dialects" are regional. People who come from Spain have a Spanish *accent*. If they come from Italy, they have an Italian *accent*. Someone who comes from the southern part of the United States has a Southern *dialect*. Most people in this industry don't know the difference, but you should still list them correctly.

Don't confuse foreign languages with accents and dialects; if you speak any foreign languages, they should also be listed. This can become very important if the film or TV show is going to be translated into a foreign language.

You might not realize how important these special abilities can be, but I have cast an actor simply because he could do the particular special ability needed for the character. That said, don't list things you don't do, and don't list things you don't do well!

Am I saying you have to be an expert? Absolutely not! The key word here is "competent." Are you competent at this certain ability? In other words, if we inquire whether you can play the piano, you don't necessarily have to read music on the spot to answer in the affirmative. But you should be able to go home, take some time, and come back and play a particular song. If when you sing in the shower the soap gets up and leaves the dish, don't list singing as a special ability. If, on the other hand, you can hold a note longer than Bank of America, then list singing in this category. If after hearing you play the guitar Van Gogh would have wanted to cut his other ear off, then it's best to leave the guitar talents off your resume.

Writing Cute Things About Yourself

A resume is no place to write cute things about yourself. Unless you have some incredible humorous, creative ability to make people laugh after viewing your resume, skip the cute things. Even if you do have that incredible talent to be creative, I'm not sure this is the place to exercise that talent.

By the term "cute," I mean statements like the following that appear especially on young performers' resumes: "loves to work with animals," "loves people," "memorizes lines quickly." They are totally unnecessary and amateurish. The place for being cute, if you need to be, and make sure you really are being cute, might be the cover letter, which will be discussed in Chapter Eleven.

Dates

Be sure not to list any dates next to anything on your resume. They give no useful information and can be detrimental. All you are doing is "dating" yourself. A resume showing the actor was extremely busy doing stage plays for fifteen years, but had hardly any work in the last four years, would make me wonder why that actor hasn't been working lately. The negatives go on from there.

Dates clutter the resume and make it harder for the director to skim. Few directors will take the time to read an entire category. Generally speaking, casting directors will take more time looking at resumes than directors will.

Local Awards

Unless you have won an Academy Award, Golden Globe Award, Emmy Award, Tony Award, or other major acting award in New York or Los Angeles, it's best not to list awards. Those high school and college awards that actors list don't mean much in the professional world of acting. They make you look somewhat amateurish on a professional acting resume, unless you're only going to be working in the smaller markets. For those markets, by all means list them. But don't list local awards on resumes in the major markets.

Order of Credits

Start with your most impressive credits first, in all categories. Some actors like to start with their smaller credits and "build." Wrong! As we skim, we'll never get to the impressive credits because almost everyone looks at only the top few credits under each category.

"Extra" Credits

Do not list any screen "extra" credits on a professional resume in New York or Los Angeles, even if you don't have any other professional acting credits. Unless directors are hiring you to be an extra, and unless this is the career path you wish to pursue, directors hiring you in those cities want to know what roles you've acted in where you "talked."

For those of you determined to list extra credits, please don't try to pass them off as speaking roles. We can see right through this one. In many of the smaller markets, it may be okay to list your extra credits. In the major markets don't list them at all! Check around with other actors in your area to see what the norm is regarding this matter.

"Extra" Work

Although this chapter is about resumes, since we're discussing the subject of extra work, we'll cover the topic here. I recommend that you do *not* do any screen extra work in Los Angeles if you want to be a professional screen actor. The idea that one starts out as an extra and then moves his way up, is generally hogwash. If you want to be a screen extra and make a career out of it, and it's true many extras earn more money over the course of the year than do speaking players because extras usually work much more, then extra work is fine. But it isn't a good idea for the actor who wants to be known as a speaking player to become associated with extra work, especially in Los Angeles.

Having said the above, there are two exceptions to this rule. Now you can join SAG by doing three days of "spear shaking" work; it is a way to get your Screen Actors Guild (SAG) card. (More on the unions in Chapter Eleven.) The three-days-of-work requirement must be with a SAG signatory company and you must be a "union extra." Many extras on TV and film sets are non-union even though the production might be a union production.

There are union and non-union vouchers. There are ratios of union to non-union extras on a union set, which are determined by the budget, location, type of media, etc. So if you're going to do extra work in order to join SAG, your job is try to get a union voucher. Endeavor to become friends with the second assistant director on a set. He is responsible for handing out the vouchers. Even if you are a non-union extra when you arrive, ask the second assistant director if he has any more "union vouchers." Sometimes a union extra won't show up. Definitely ask!

When you go to join SAG, however, the voucher will not be enough proof for eligibility. You'll need pay-stubs for that since copies of checks are also unacceptable. SAG suggests that a performer should wait at least 45 days before submitting original pay-stubs to the Guild. (See Eligibility Requirements for joining SAG in Appendix E.)

You'll find that obtaining extra work isn't easy by any stretch of the imagination. It is sometimes almost as hard to get to meet the people who cast extras as the people who cast speaking roles. This can take time away from your getting in to see the people who cast speaking roles. So, if you want to be a professional speaking actor you should only be considering extra work as a way to get those three days' work.

The second reason to do extra work in Los Angeles is that you get on a set for a few days to learn something about what takes place on an actual shoot. The only problem with getting a few days of extra work and earning pretty good money is, it becomes habit-forming. Being on a set and seeing many stars is exciting. But, you're taking valuable time away from your goals if you want to eventually be a speaking actor. I detest the phrase "Once an extra, always an extra," but it comes about because of the above.

I'll often hear actors talk about how they did a "featured extra" part. That generally means they did a piece of business in a scene; they moved a prop, etc. Or they'll mention that they actually stood next to Brad Pitt in a scene. If you were looking for a surgeon, would you go to the guy who "stood right next to a surgeon once during actual surgery"? The same applies here. Extra parts in big films might be impressive in Omaha, but I can't imagine anyone in Los Angeles being impressed by your extra credits if you want to be an actor who speaks.

However, since New York is a theater town, it isn't as detrimental to your career to do screen extra work there if you're just starting out. Many actors who are looking for theater acting jobs supplement their incomes with extra work. However, as stated above, extra work in New York, as well as Los Angeles, should *not* be listed on your professional resume.

As for the cities beyond the main production centers of Los Angeles and New York, many times out-of-town production companies will be likely to cast extra and smaller speaking roles from local talent. Having such screen extra credits on your resume will at least show that you've been on a set, which is generally very important to most directors. As always, check with other actors, and especially agents, in your particular area to see what the norm is concerning the listing of extra credits.

Extra work for the stage is almost nonexistent. When there is a need for non-speaking stage roles, they are usually filled by understudies for larger roles and not considered extra. Understudy work is very beneficial and highly recommended. Think of the times a star has not been able to fulfill her duties on a particular night, and the understudy has "gone on" and gotten her big break.

(At SAG, there have been constant discussions about either making the requirements for joining the Guild through extra work more restrictive or eventually dropping the eligibility into SAG by doing any extra work entirely. It would be best to check with SAG on what the current status is with regards to this matter.)

What to Do with Your Resume

When you finish composing your resume you might find that it has much less information on it than you had originally imagined. Every professionally working actor had a first professional acting job, and you'll be no different. No one started out with a lot of professional acting credits. As time goes by, you'll accumulate more credits and your resume will look more and more impressive.

Type your resume very neatly. A practice that some actors use so that their resume doesn't look too permanent, is to leave off a recent credit, on purpose, when typing and to write it in, in pencil. Their intent here is to make it appear as though they are so busy they can hardly keep up with their resume. Years ago, there was some merit to this, but with the advent of computers this idea seems less effective nowadays.

Duplicate as many copies of your resume as you have headshots. If you're just starting out in Los Angeles or New York, you'll need two hundred to three hundred to begin with. I am suggesting that you'll probably be sending your photo and resume, known as a "package" in the industry, to many agents in the city in which you plan to work.

You'll probably get fewer responses than you anticipate. Even after you obtain an agent you'll need to give him many photos and resumes to send to potential employers.

Staple your resume to the back of your headshot so that when you turn the photo over you can read your resume (in other words, back-to-back). If your photo is printed on 8 x 10 stock and your resume on 8½ x 11 paper, trim the paper to match the photo size so that you don't have excess paper hanging below your photo.

Use four staples, one in each corner. Paper clipping resumes is a no-no. Agents, and eventually casting directors and directors, looking over your photos and resumes very quickly are likely to get your photo separated from your resume if they aren't stapled together. I mentioned earlier the times I was unable to call back a certain actor in an audition because his headshot wasn't attached to his resume and we had no way of contacting the actor without doing some research.

And please staple the photo to the resume *before* you come to the actual audition. This may sound obvious, yet actors do show up in the lobby asking for a stapler, or worse, asking us when they come into the actual audition room. We usually don't have one. Some actors glue their resume to the back of their photo. If it's your agent's wish, then go ahead, but I wouldn't suggest this. No, we don't have the glue on hand, either.

The problem with gluing is that, over time, the glue weakens and the photo and resume can become separated. This happens often in auditions. Heat gets to your photo and resume and the package will ripple. In my opinion, gluing the resume to the back of the photo gives the package too much of a permanent look. For the same reason, don't have your resume printed directly on the back of your headshot. This makes it appear as though you don't work very often and that you don't think you're going to have a job (hence, change in resume) for some time.

Now that you have a professional photo and resume, we'll move on to the person with the most important influence on your acting career outside of yourself—YOUR AGENT.

Sample Basic Stage Resume

JACK SMITH
Equity, SAG, AFTRA

Height: 5´8˝		Joe Smith Agency
Weight: 135		2000 Some Street
Eyes: Hazel		Hollywood, CA 00000
Hair: Brown		555-555-5555
		(e-mail and/or website
		address here)

STAGE ROLES:

Fiddler on the Roof	Fyedka	The Theatre, Miami
The Miser	Harpegon	Guthrie Theatre, Chicago
The Guest	Bill	The Dinner Theatre, Denver
The Play	John	The Dinner Theatre, Denver
The Odd Couple	Felix (u/s)	The Center Theatre, Houston

FILM:

Mr. Smith	Co-Star	Bill Smith Productions
The Drowning Ship	Feature	Jim Robards Productions

TELEVISION:

NYPD Blues	Guest-Star	NBC
ER	Principal	NBC

COMMERCIALS:
List Available Upon Request

THEATRICAL TRAINING:

The Actors' Center	Bill Rogers	Philadelphia
Actorsinfobooth	Linda Fionte	Ft. Lauderdale, Florida
Aspire Talent	Sharon Bell	Denver

SPECIAL ABILITIES:
Water-skiing
Fencing
Horseback Riding
Piano

Sample Basic TV & Film Resume

BILL RAY
SAG, AFTRA, Equity

Height: 6´1˝	Joe Smith Agency
Weight: 185	2000 Some Street
Eyes: Blue	Hollywood, CA 00000
Hair: Blond	555-555-5555
	(e-mail and/or website
	address here)

TAPE AVAILABLE

Film:

The Clam That Ate Gramps	Principal	Arts Studios
The Mystique	Featured	Tom Productions

TELEVISION:

Friends	Co-Star	NBC
Will & Grace	Guest-Star	NBC

COMMERCIALS:
List Available Upon Request

STAGE ROLES:

Fiddler on the Roof	Fyedka	The Theatre, Miami
The Miser	Harpegon	Guthrie Theatre, Chicago
The Guest	Bill	The Dinner Theatre, Denver
The Odd Couple	Felix (u/s)	The Center Theatre, Houston

THEATRICAL TRAINING:

Performing Arts Center	John Foreman	New York
Performance Workshops	Jill Powell	Los Angeles
Tom Baker Workshops	Tom Baker	Chicago

SPECIAL ABILITIES:
Tennis
Guitar
Skydiving

CHAPTER ELEVEN

Do Obtain the Best Agent Possible

One day a shark was seen swimming the shores of Los Angeles in Santa Monica Bay. This particular shark was eating everyone in the Bay. Then it came to a Hollywood agent and swam right by him—you know, professional courtesy.

Yes, it's true, some agents are sharks. In this business, however, you need a shark. Like it or not, agents will be around as long as someone else has talent. Agents have more inside information than a surgeon. So now that you have two important tools of the acting profession—your photo and resume—it's time to start searching for a shark.

There are some good agents and there are some not-so-good agents. But an agent that is not good for one actor might be great for another, like the fellow who might be a horrible date for most of you women, but will be good for somebody else. In many respects, searching for the right agent is kind of like searching for the right mate: You'll probably go through quite a few before you find a really good match. Then some day that match won't work any longer and you'll have to find another match—kind of like marriage in Hollywood.

What an Agent Can (and Can't) Do for You

Before you begin your search for an agent, you may as well know that your agent can't promise you work. There are no guarantees. Legitimate agents won't give you a guarantee that they'll send you on even one audition. They have no way of knowing how many, if any, auditions they can get you into. Your agent's job is not to get you work—that's your job!

Your agent's job is to get your package into the hands of as many directors and casting directors as possible; then to follow up your package with phone calls trying to get you on the audition. I use the term "agent" whether you may be dealing with an individual agent, or with one working for a larger agency. In the latter case, more than one agent may be working on your behalf. In either case, in industry jargon, you'd refer to your agent, in the singular.

Once you obtain an acting job, your agent's job is to negotiate your contracts and salary. This puts protection between you and the director and producers of the show. No director or producer wants to say directly to an actor, "You're not worth a million for this film," or "You're not a big enough 'name' to have 'above the title' billing." We have to work with that actor throughout the entire project, so we don't want to start off the relationship on such a negative note.

Let your agent do the dirty work. That's what they do. And generally agents are better business people than are actors. When an actor gets involved in his own negotiations, with the accompanying emotions and egos, it spells trouble for us on a set. The actor has to be free to only worry about his performance during an actual shoot.

Who to Contact for Representation

In Los Angeles you can't exist without an agent . In New York, without one, it is a little easier to exist, but I strongly recommend you start looking for an agent no matter what city you're operating from. You have no way of knowing everything that is being cast in that city. Even if you had a direct source of such information, you still wouldn't have the power to get yourself into most of the auditions. Obtaining a bit of information about a casting doesn't do you much good if you don't have an agent who can get you in the door.

In Los Angeles people who proudly say they don't have an agent and are freelancing are telling you one of two things: either they can't get an agent, or they are too naive to know they need one. They are making a grave mistake and their future will eventually show them how foolish they have been. For appearance's sake you need an agent. No one takes you very seriously if you aren't represented. I'll admit that almost every feature film, television show, and commercial I've directed was work I obtained myself from referrals. However, I still need an agent to be taken seriously. And, yes, directors, producers, casting directors, directors of photography, and others have representation also. We're all in the same boat as far as the agent routine goes.

When searching for someone to contact for representation, you must be careful to look for a legitimate agent. Many people move to the big city to become actors and, unfortunately, being newcomers, will be ripped off by con artists. This happens when people first get to the big city because they are so starstruck they'll fall for almost any scheme.

"What's a couple hundred bucks to make me a star?" they think. If it were that easy, everyone and their grandmother would be a star. Review the following information to help you learn what steps to take in your search, and, at the very least, how to avoid throwing your money away on doomed-to-fail methods.

Any agent who tries to separate you from your money before you land a job isn't the type of agent you want! I'm referring to accepted practices in the professional acting industry. A legitimate agent won't get any money until you do; he'll get a percentage of your earnings—not a flat fee. If an agent asks you for money up-front, put your hand over your pocket, hold your wallet or purse very tightly, and run like hell. An exception to this applies in smaller cities outside of the major shooting centers, where some agencies also have schools. This is a perfectly accepted practice in the smaller markets, while it is not accepted as legitimate for an agent in the major markets of Los Angeles and New York. But, again, the agent shouldn't ask you for money in exchange for representation. What they might do in the smaller markets is ask you to train for a fee, to better your skills before taking you on as a client. Whether you want to study at their school and be represented by them or move to another agency is up to you.

In the show business trade papers, you'll read all kinds of ads for companies calling themselves video casting services or a similar name, that promise to make you a demo reel which they'll supposedly show to the studios. Unfortunately, few, if any, of these demos will ever make it to any studio. Ads for these companies say they will put your photo and resume online for directors and casting directors to view. Check these out very carefully before investing your money. In the real world, we cast through agents. Many agents, especially commercial agents, now use an online service for submitting actors photos called "L.A. Casting." But it is for agents and managers only. So we're still using your agent's services.

My experience, and that of other professionals in the business, suggests that anyone who promises to get you work as an actor is either naive or is trying to rip you off—probably the latter. No legitimate agent, or no legitimate anything or anyone, will promise you the landing of a professional acting job.

Determining Which Agents to Contact

When you're first starting out it's not so much you choosing an agent as the agent choosing you. I know it sounds all "artsy-fartsy" to say that the agent works for you and that you hire the agent, even though in theory, this is correct because you pay the agent a percentage of your salary. But for the beginner, in most cases you're looking for an agent to choose you rather than the other way around. Once you are well-established, the roles reverse.

In the major markets, including Los Angeles and New York, you want an agent who is either affiliated with SAG and/or franchised by AFTRA, or one who is a member of the Association of Talent Agents (ATA) or of the National Association of Talent Representatives (NATR). Modeling agents and print agents, even in Los Angeles and

New York, do not associate themselves with any union or association, so you're on your own there.

It used to be that any agent who wasn't franchised by the union(s) wasn't legit. Currently, however, ATA and NATR agents do not have agreements with SAG (although they do with AFTRA). Still, in the major markets, including Los Angeles and New York, you should only deal with agents who are either affiliated with SAG, or are AFTRA franchised, or ones who are members of the ATA or NATR.

ATA and NATR agency contracts are vastly different from standard SAG agency contracts. Members of SAG are strongly encouraged to contact the Guild before signing any contract that is foreign to them. SAG members who sign other agency contracts are doing so outside of the scope of protection SAG has traditionally provided.

When I refer to "union agents," I will be referring to those agents who are affiliated with SAG. When I refer to "union/association agents," I will be referring to agents who were formerly franchised by SAG, and/or are currently AFTRA franchised, or are members of the ATA or NATR.

The rules of the union and union/association agents govern percentages that an agent can legally take from your wages; agreements between you and the agent on how long you'll work together; what the agent's obligation is to you; and what your obligation is to that agent. (This is covered more fully later in this chapter and in Chapter Twelve.)

For those going into stage work, you'll want a union agent who is franchised by Actors' Equity Association (commonly known as "Equity"). If your career is headed in the direction of TV, film, and commercials, you want a union or union/association agent. You can obtain lists of union and union/association agents from the appropriate unions and associations either by mail, in person, or online. NATR does not have a website. (For website addresses of the unions and the ATA, see Appendix A. For street addresses and phone numbers of the union offices, see Appendices B, C, and D.)

If you're about to do business with an agent who isn't on the appropriate list, you can still call the organization which has jurisdiction over your particular field and check that agent out, or check the appropriate organization's website. It's possible it might be a new agency and not appear on your list yet. The lists of agents you obtain directly from the unions and associations include the agency's name, office address, and phone number.

Helpful Publications

In the smaller cities outside of Los Angeles and New York, you might as well submit your package to all the agents in the city in which you plan to work. If you plan to work in Los Angeles or New York, to submit your photo and resume to every agent is costly, though you may eventually end up doing this. Certain agents do cater to specific physical types, and you can check this out. In Los Angeles, you can obtain a copy of the *Academy Players Directory* (www.acadpd.org) or go and view a copy at the Academy of Motion Picture Arts and Sciences located at 1313 North Vine, in Hollywood. Their phone number is 310-247-3000. By looking through this "book," which shows photos of actors and lists their agents, you'll get an idea who handles what types of actors. AMPAS publishes it three times a year in four volumes.

For a small fee an actor can have his name and photo, along with the name of his agent, printed in this publication. The *Academy Players Directory* requires that an actor be a member of one of the acting unions to be listed. Many casting directors and directors refer to this publication, so once you're a member of any of the acting unions, it's important for you to list with this publication if you're in Los Angeles or New York. In fact, it is imperative. Outside of these two areas, many theatrical and commercial agents have a "headsheet"—a booklet of photos of their actors. In this case, each actor on the headsheet will usually be charged a nominal fee for the printing of the booklet.

To give you an idea of how important it is for you to be listed in the *Academy Players Directory*, notice that well-known stars and celebrities put their photos in this publication. When an agent doesn't have time to get a photo to me of a particular actor, I might ask, "What Academy page?" The agent knows this means I want the page number where that actor's photo can be located in the *Directory*.

Another way to find out about certain agents is from other actors. Most actors have plenty of ideas about which agents are good for new people and which aren't. The very best way to learn about agents is to obtain a copy of *The Agencies* from the largest drama bookstore in the world—Samuel French, which has stores in Los Angeles and New York, Larry Edmunds Bookstore in Los Angeles, or The Drama Book Shop in New York.

This is a very inexpensive publication and invaluable to the beginning and experienced actor. One edition lists all the agencies in Los Angeles and a separate edition for those in New York. It even lists the individual names of all the agents in each agency. All those listed are union and union/association agents.

The Agencies also specifies what physical types each agent handles. If a particular agent typically handles actors that could pick up Winnebagos looking for small change, and you were once beat up by a Quaker, perhaps this agency isn't right for you. Some would argue that such an agency is exactly where you want to be because you'd be different from everyone else in the agency and you wouldn't have as much competition within the agency. This is true to a certain extent. The problem would be that, if I'm looking for a Baywatch type and you're the type that could model duffel-bags but your agency is known for bathing beauties, your agency probably would never be contacted when it comes to casting that role.

I can't stress enough the importance of putting the actual name of the individual agent on your package when you submit it. Without an addressee designated on your package to an agency, who knows in whose circular file (wastepaper basket) it will find itself. Do you take it very seriously when you receive mail addressed to "Occupant"? A package sent to an agency without naming a particular agent, makes it appear as though you are just sending your package to everyone on the list—which might be the truth—and that you are not very picky about who represents you.

You can save yourself a lot of money by following *The Agencies* because it describes in detail who should submit to a particular agent and who shouldn't. Some agencies only handle stars and for someone just beginning, it probably wouldn't be advantageous to submit to that agency.

Contacting the Agents

Once you've decided which agents to contact, it doesn't mean you should just call an agent on the phone or drop by for coffee. If you call an agent on the phone out of the clear blue, that agent is only going to tell you to send him a photo and resume. What have you achieved? You've wasted his time and yours, and you haven't made the best first impression.

The easiest way to get in to see an agent is to have a friend who is a director, casting director, producer, or another actor who is signed with that same agency recommend you. "Industry referrals" as they are called are certainly taken the most seriously.

The only, and I mean only, drawback to industry referrals is that if I phone an agent for an actor, the agent would most likely have the actor come in for an interview, but he might not really be interested in the actor. Just because a director referred him, the agent may even take the actor on as a client. But will he work for you? An agent is only going to work for you if he really believes in your work. You don't want an agent to take you on as a favor or because of outside influence. I believe an agent seeing you perform in some play, workshop, or whatever and being so excited about you that he interviews you based on that performance is the best of all possible worlds.

So, the question arises, if you know someone who can refer you should you take that opportunity? Absolutely! Yes! Yes! Yes! Just make sure the agent then sees you perform in something after signing you, so that he will become excited about your acting abilities.

Mailing your package, accompanied by a cover letter, to the agent's office is the most common way to contact an agent. Sending your photo and resume without a cover letter makes it appear as though you are sending mass mailings to all the agents. Even though there's nothing wrong with doing this, you don't want to be so obvious about it.

Keep the cover letter short and to the point because agents are very busy people. When most directors, myself included, receive long letters we tend to not read them. It's the same with agents. Long letters are much more likely to end up in the circular file, unread, than short ones. Long explanations aren't needed. Every agent knows why you're sending them your package. If you have some film on yourself, you should mention that in the cover letter. (A sample cover letter is presented in this chapter, but it is only a sample; you should construct your own letter.)

Once you have sent your package to agents, if they don't call you within a week or so, phone them. It probably means they aren't interested if they don't call you within that time frame, but sometimes agents do get very busy and forget to phone you, or you're not on their priority list that week. The best time to phone an agent is late in the afternoon; try around five-thirty or six o'clock. Generally, I have found that's the best time to try to talk to people in this business, because the secretary has usually left and the person you're trying to contact might be answering his own phone.

You can reason it through: In the morning hours agents are busy submitting actors for roles, making phone calls to casting directors to see who they can get into auditions, making rounds at the studios, and so on. If you phone at that time, your chances of getting an agent on the phone are even slimmer than slim. Avoid phoning on

Mondays or Fridays. I would suggest trying agents on a Tuesday, Wednesday, or Thursday.

When you reach someone in the agent's office, probably a secretary, simply identify yourself and explain that you sent your photo and resume to them on such-and-such a date. You probably won't get any further than that with that call. But you're going to keep trying.

Remember my earlier caution: Be nice to secretaries. A secretary is many times the one person that separates you from the people you want to meet. I believe that the way to have a great marriage is to have a very short memory—secretaries don't! If you aren't nice to them, they'll remember you. It is their job to both separate you, and screen you from, the person in the back room. Secretaries are the gatekeepers to the people you want to meet. And don't think the secretary won't talk to the agent about who was naughty and who was nice.

Even if the secretary is rude to you, be nice to her. When you ask to speak to Mr. Big, you'll probably be located somewhere between "Sorry, he's tied up now," and "Sorry, he no longer works here." Ask for an appointment anyway and the secretary may say something like, "How about never? Is 'never' good for you?" In this case be nice and move on.

It's almost automatic for an agent or secretary to tell you on the phone that he is "not looking for new people"; that's only a half-truth. When an agent thinks he can make money off you, he's "looking." And believe me, if Tom Cruise calls, that agent will be looking for new people. When an agent uses the term "new people," he isn't referring to how long an actor has or has not been in the business. He is saying he has as many clients as he can handle and is not interested in seeing people he doesn't already represent; in other words, actors "new" to that agent.

It won't hurt you to realize that if you send your package to every single agency in Los Angeles, for example, the odds are extremely slim of hearing from any of them on that first mailing, and possibly your second or third, for that matter. Don't let it bother you. Obtaining an agent is one of the most frustrating processes of the acting profession. Getting a bona fide agent to represent you is like working on a 3,000-piece jigsaw puzzle that's all sky. And, if it'll make you feel any better, directors and producers have the same frustrations with obtaining representation.

Should You "Drop by" Agents' Offices?

You can just drop by some agencies to leave your package. Most likely you're only going to come in contact with a secretary. But if you make a good impression, that secretary might, and I emphasize might, put in a good word for you. Don't stay long and chat! Don't ask to see the agent(s) in the office. Don't ask for an audition. Simply drop off your package and ask that person to give it to Mrs. Big Wig.

Some agencies are so small that they don't have a secretary, so you might be handing your package to an actual agent! Even then, you can't expect great results from the drop-by method, but it is a step ahead of mailing your package. Some office buildings, where agents' offices are located, for security purposes (especially since 9/11) have guards to keep you from doing this. As long as you are polite, you have nothing to lose.

The SAG Conservatory

Beyond your "package," there are other ways to be seen. The Screen Actors Guild has the SAG Conservatory where you can meet agents and casting directors. Fortunately, these workshops are free. Unfortunately, they are for members of SAG only, except in the case of a minor. Under fifteen years of age permits you to join the SAG Conservatory whether you're a SAG member or not. Members of SAG, or those actors under the age of fifteen, should contact their local SAG office to find out about these very worthwhile workshops.

Performing in Showcase Plays/Workshops

No matter what your emphasis is, you should get into some plays that are being performed in the city in which you plan to work as an actor. If the purpose of the showcase play is to show your talents, don't get in one that is very far out of town. Most industry people don't like to travel far from the center of the industry. In Los Angeles, few agents, if any, will travel to Santa Barbara to see you perform. Likewise, in New York, few agents would travel to Trenton, New Jersey to see your play.

Many casting directors and agents attend plays, especially ones that get good reviews in the trades. So, where the photo-resume routine might not work for you—the odds are actually stacked very much against you—many agents do get out to see plays and attend "industry night" workshops.

In Los Angeles the most common type of showcase play is called the "L.A. 99 Seat Plan," and in New York it is called a "Showcase Code" production. Both the L.A. 99 Seat Plan and the Showcase Code productions serve the same purpose, though the technical contents of the codes differ. You'll still hear some people refer to the L.A. 99 Seat Plan by its old name, "Equity Waiver plays."

Both of these types of plays, though there are some variations of the Showcase Code, are staged in theatres of "99 seats or less," and are produced specifically to help artists showcase their respective talents. For this reason, the play is under Equity rules, though the actors are rarely paid. Equity members may also audition and perform in these showcase plays. (Note: Acting in these plays does *not* fulfill the eligibility requirements for joining Equity.)

Off-Off-Broadway is any production in New York City that is not Broadway or Off-Broadway. Basically, the term refers to any theatre in New York City that is completely non-Equity. Whereas both Equity and non-Equity actors can perform in Showcase Code productions, Equity members may not perform in typical Off-Off-Broadway productions.

As far as Los Angeles and New York are concerned, less experienced actors are in the non-Equity productions and for this reason, usually fewer agents are in the audience. You can obtain information about showcase plays in Los Angeles from *Backstage West* and in New York from *Backstage*. Many of the smaller markets don't have these professional showcase plays, but do have community theatre plays, which, at least in those cities, serve the same purpose.

Once you are cast in a showcase play, send notices via mail to agents about your performance. In addition, fax a copy of that same notice to their offices. Send flyers to casting directors and casting directors' assistants. Sending notices to the assistants is extremely important, because many times they are the ones who attend the plays. Be brief: Simply invite the agent, provide the address of the theatre and the dates of the performances, and mention that you are seeking representation. (See sample notice in this chapter.)

Make very sure that the agent or other industry professional you invite will have complimentary tickets. Don't expect anyone in this industry to pay to see you perform. Most showcase theatres will admit industry people (agents, producers, directors, casting directors, etc.) for free.

A good idea is to include your package along with the invitation. Better yet, have postcards printed up with your photo on the front. Sometimes when agents see a large envelope they toss it into the trash if they're not seeking new talent, because they suspect that it's a photo and resume. Postcards are quicker to view since we don't have to tear open envelopes. (Postcards are also great for thanking people after you've met with them.)

Only a small percentage, if any, of the agents whom you invite will actually attend the play, but that's to be expected. Take comfort that other members of the cast will also have sent out notices; this will broaden the number of agents in the audience. (Note: If you are cast in one of these plays be sure to have a plentiful supply of photos and resumes with you—*every night of the performance*. You never know who might be in the audience, afterwards someone might ask you for your photo and resume.)

Don't be offended if an industry person leaves at intermission. I have never done this, but we do know in the first few minutes what we need to know. Also, that industry professional has probably been up since very early in the morning and will have to do the same the next morning. If this happens to you, it is not a bad sign by any stretch of the imagination.

In the larger markets, there are "industry-night" showcases that are also very popular. Many industry people would rather attend one of these than a full-length play, although you should also perform in plays. With this type of showcase, an industry professional can see many actors perform in a very short period of time (and eat some really good food!), as opposed to seeing only a few actors over the course of an entire evening.

They are referred to as "industry night" showcases because that's just what they are—showcases where the actors do a short scene in front of people in the industry. Many of us have a hard time sitting through full-length plays in order to see only a handful of actors. We would rather see more actors doing shorter scenes. It maximizes our time.

The industry-night showcases charge a fee to the actor. I have a problem with an agent or casting director charging an actor just to be seen, but these showcases/workshops can be helpful. What you're doing, in effect, is paying for a meeting or audition with an agent or casting director. The subject makes me cringe when it comes up, but an "actor's gotta do what an actor's gotta do."

Despite my dislike of this practice of paying a fee to audition, it is a way of being seen, so if you are going to do it, find some good showcases to demonstrate your talents. If you took the amount of money spent for the showcase and spent the same sending out your photos and resumes, how many casting directors/agents would you then get to personally meet, much less perform in front of? If it's a good, well-known gig, then it makes sense financially to perform in industry night showcases.

If you do a scene for an industry-night showcase, make sure the scene is short! Three minutes or less is plenty of time for everyone to get an idea of your talents. Choose a scene to perform that we haven't seen thousands of times. One from *The Odd Couple* or *Our Town* should be avoided at all costs; even though they are great plays, we've seen scenes from them too many times.

Keep Trying!

The main thing is, don't get discouraged. Very few actors obtain an agent within the first few months after moving to Los Angeles or New York. If you don't succeed on the first try, go through the list of agents again several months later. The agents probably won't remember your first attempt, although the secretaries probably will.

Why send so many packages to the same agents over a period of time? Because situations change—both yours and the agents'. Because many agents take clients by physical type—so many all-American, so many street-kid, so many prostitute types—maybe when you sent your first package to that agent he already had plenty of clients that fit your type. A later package might arrive at a time when he could use someone like you, when some of those actors that fit your type have moved on to other agents.

Agents turn down actors for other reasons, as well. You might not be taken as a client because your credits might not be up to the agent's standards. She may not handle you because you're not a member of SAG, or, in the case of a stage agent, Equity. An agent may simply be too busy representing established actors with household names, and trying to get a newcomer in the door would probably consume more of his time than it would be worth. After all, agents are in this business to make money.

Big vs. Small Agent

A "big" agent is one who handles established actors and who has more clout with casting directors, directors, and producers. Generally, "big" is no indication of how many clients the agent actually handles. If you get to be handled by the same agent who handles Julia Roberts, then you'll have a much better chance of getting interviewed for a Julie Roberts' movie than if you were with a smaller agent. The more stars the agent handles, the more pull he has. But, the bigger the agent the more competition you have within your own agency to be submitted for roles.

Any agent handling someone like Julia Roberts will probably work much harder for "Julia" than for someone less established. When you're first starting out in Los Angeles or New York, it's usually better to be handled by a "smaller" agent. The smaller agent can't sit around and rely on star clients to pay his rent; he has to hustle for his clients.

Obtaining the right size agent is a balancing act. The bigger agent has more clout, but is less inclined to work for someone just starting out. The smaller agent may not have the clout to get you into most auditions, but he may work much harder for you. You can see how it works. And that balancing act will stick around with you for your entire career. Actors aren't alone here. Directors and producers have agents, too, and we have the same balancing act to worry about as you do. The best bet is to balance out the two things—the power of one agent versus the interest and excitement level towards you by the other agent—and decide which you prefer.

Once you start chatting with other actors and you learn more about the business, you'll begin to know who handles whom. If you want to work in the smaller markets, it's very unlikely that any agent will be handling a stable of stars, so check with other actors in your city to get an idea which agents seem to be obtaining the most work for their actors.

Be persistent! *There is a direct correlation between the number of door-bells you ring and the number of vacuum cleaners you sell—no matter how effective the product or how good the salesman.* You don't have to be brilliant to work in this industry, but you do have to have incredible staying power.

The Importance and the Role of the Acting Unions

There are *good* reasons why we discussed the importance of obtaining an agent who is a union or union/association agent earlier. In the major markets, the legit studios, producers, directors, casting directors, and others do not negotiate with agents who aren't affiliated with SAG as union agents, or union/association agents. Likewise, professional theatre producers usually don't negotiate with non-Equity agents.

You need a union or union/association agent because these agents make their money by obtaining work for you. It is to their advantage to work hard for you. Agents in the major markets of Los Angeles and New York who aren't union or union/association agents usually make their money from charging actors to sign up with them. Why should these non-legit agents work hard to obtain work for their clients? They're making easy money just signing up actors.

The unions and associations protect you when dealing with their agents. If you have a grievance to take up with one of these agents over any matter, you can contact the appropriate union or association and its staff will help you and the agent resolve the matter.

It's important for you to become a member of the appropriate acting union(s) if you wish to work in the major markets. If you are presently working in a right-to-work state and never plan to move to a bigger market, then you might want to stay non-union to build up your credit list, assuming that there is more non-union work than union in your present market. In the major markets you're considered a professional actor only after you've become a member of a professional acting union.

On Union Affiliation

Your primary concern as an actor is with SAG, AFTRA, and Equity, the three unions I mention in the chapter on resumes. A quick overview of all the performers' unions before you start searching for an agent might be useful to you.

Five performers unions make up the Associated Actors and Artists of America (commonly referred to as the "4As")—SAG, AFTRA, Equity, AGVA, and AGMA, which are briefly sketched below. If you have been a member of any 4A for at least a year and have worked under that union's jurisdiction and your dues are current, you are eligible to join another 4A. (Note: If you are a member of any of the 4As and you join another 4A union, the initiation fee and dues stated below may be reduced. Check with the appropriate union.) All figures below are subject to change so check each union's website for possible changes.

- Screen Actors Guild (SAG) (www.sag.org) is the union having jurisdiction over performers working in feature films, filmed TV shows, filmed commercials, and industrial films. One can become a member by being cast in a filmed union production, TV or otherwise, as a speaking player, or as a stunt player even if one doesn't speak. One can also become a member by having at least three days of "extra" (commonly referred to as "background player") work on a SAG production. (See detailed discussion in Chapter Ten).

  The initiation fee for joining SAG is $1,310, plus $50 for the first semi-annual basic dues payment; total joining fee is $1,360. Fees may be lower in certain branch offices.

  For a complete understanding of all the technical ins and outs of membership into SAG, you might want to pick up a copy of the complete "Basic Agreement" from any SAG office. (Specific eligibility requirements for joining SAG are contained in Appendix E.)

- American Federation of Television and Radio Artists (AFTRA) (www.aftra.org) has jurisdiction over performers working in live and taped TV shows, taped commercials and industrials, television and radio news, sports and weather, radio programming and commercials, sound recordings, interactive CD-ROM, and other new media. The only requirement for joining AFTRA is payment of its initiation fee and dues; the standard joining fee is $1,200, plus $58 for the first six months dues.

- Actors' Equity Association (AEA) (www.actorsequity.org) is the union having jurisdiction over performers and stage managers in play productions. The most common way to become eligible to join Equity is by being cast, or obtaining a stage manager's position, in an Equity stage production. One can also become a member by joining the Equity Membership Candidate Program (EMC) at a participating Equity theatre, or by virtue of prior membership in a 4As performing arts sister union. (See specific eligibility requirements for joining Equity in Appendices F and G.) The initiation fee for joining is $1,000, plus $118 in semi-annual dues. Working dues are 2 percent of weekly earnings, which max out at $150,000.

- American Guild of Variety Artists (AGVA) is the union having jurisdiction over a wide variety of *live* performers, ranging from circus clowns to nightclub performers. The only requirement for joining is that you are a working performer, or a member of another 4A union, and can pay the initiation fee of $750, plus your first quarterly dues, which vary depending on your first contract. If you have a contract when you join, your first quarterly dues will be $24.

- American Guild of Musical Artists (AGMA) is the union having jurisdiction over opera singers, classical dancers, and choral singers. The initiation fee is $500; the first six months' dues are $39; total joining fee is $539. Dues are $39.00 every six months. Every time you work on a show under AGMA's jurisdiction, 2 percent of your salary is deducted as "working dues."

For obtaining an agent, it carries much more weight to be a member of SAG, since anyone can join AFTRA. SAG is the union you should be the most concerned about if you're interested in screen acting. In other words, if you went down to AFTRA and paid your money to join, that wouldn't fulfill the eligibility requirements for joining SAG through AFTRA. If you're a member of AFTRA and have spoken a line of dialogue under an AFTRA contract, you would then be eligible to join SAG one year after you joined AFTRA.

By becoming a member of SAG, screen agents know that you've probably worked professionally in front of the motion picture or TV camera. Working in front of the camera is obviously much different from working on the stage. For the same reason most directors are reluctant to see you for auditions if you aren't a member of SAG, most agents would be reluctant to take you on as a client.

Taft-Hartley

You do not have to join a union immediately after you obtain a job. You can "Taft-Hartley" your first job. The "Taft-Hartley" law states that you can work a certain amount of time on a union job without having to join that union. Some unions interpret this law differently, but as it typically applies to the acting unions, you can work up to 30 *calendar* days on your first union job without joining the appropriate union. On your second job, or on any job that continues over 30 calendar days, you must join the relevant union if you want to work on a union show under that union. (In right-to-work states this law does not apply because a union cannot enforce the joining of a union in those states.)

Okay, so now that you know the basic requirements for union affiliation, you may be dismayed. Not only does it cost money, which you may not have, you discover that you can't get the union credentials you need without having a job first. And the agents are reluctant to help you find a job if you're not a member of the appropriate union(s). The situation is not as desperate as you might think. Your performance in showcase plays, workshops, as well as having film on yourself can be helpful.

Submitting Film on Yourself

If you plan to pursue a career in TV, film, and commercials, then doing plays is important, but it's even more important to have film on yourself, as I touched on earlier. Having videotape or a DVD of yourself is referred to as "film on yourself" in everyday jargon, but on your resume should be referred to as "Tape Available," if your scene is on videotape. If your work is put on DVD, then print "DVD Available" instead. This presentation of your work is also known as a "demo reel," "demo," or just plain "reel." These terms are interchangeable.

There are many advantages to having a reel. Directors can watch your tape at their convenience—even at home while munching on popcorn. A reel isn't taking our time away during the busy hours of the day by having us make an appointment with you that we may or may not be able to keep.

Second, a reel goes beyond watching an actor on stage, which only shows that agent your acting ability on stage. The reel not only shows your acting ability in front of the camera, but also shows him how you react to the camera and how you play-off another actor. And it will show him how well you do or don't photograph.

Television, film, and commercials are a *visual* medium, not auditory, as is stage. Whether we're watching an actual live audition or a recorded one, we're watching the person who is reacting more than the person speaking. Watch television and films very closely and notice how much more time the person reacting has on camera than the person speaking. In good situation-comedy a given line may get a laugh, but the reaction to that line will usually pick up the bigger laugh.

The director is going to pay particular attention to how you "play off" the other actor. Let's say one actor has to say to the other, "Tom, you're so ugly, I can't stand it." When you watch that line in the finished product, the camera will probably be on the person speaking the line when he says, "Tom, you're so . . . . ," but before he can say, ". . . ugly I can't stand it," the image will cut to the other person to pick up his reaction to, " . . . . ugly I can't stand it." This is an example of how we "cut." And it's important for the actor to give us those "play-offs" for editing purposes.

In one scene of a film I was directing at one of the major studios, we had a "dead body" in the street. The suits had spent a lot of money on that fake body, so they were pretty proud of it. (Why we didn't get an actor to play the dead body is another question.) After I had shot a short take of the body, I started to move on to the reaction shots.

The suits weren't happy, saying such things as, "Shoot the dead body . . . . It looks so real . . . . Shoot more shots because we spent some bucks on him . . . . etc." They missed the point of the scene. It's not the dead body that is interesting, it's other people's reaction to it that makes it interesting. A policeman putting his arm around a family member and walking him away would be interesting. Or someone looking down at the body and covering his face would really tell the scene. The body (pardon the pun) is a dead shot. Once it has been shown, it's not going anywhere and it's not going to do anything interesting.

That's why screen directors would rather see you perform on a recorded medium rather than just in a monologue. And most agents understand this. A monologue doesn't tell an agent or screen director how easy or hard it will be to "cut" your performance. The director has to have something to "cut to," and if the actor shows expression only when he is speaking his own dialogue, then there will be trouble in the editing room. There isn't time to teach acting on a set, as I said, and we expect to see the expressions in your live or recorded audition. I know I said this isn't a book about "how to act," but the director in me makes me mention it anyway.

It would be an exception to the above if you had performed a monologue in a film or TV show. This would be very rare, but it must be mentioned. Even so, hopefully you have other footage where you are playing-off other actors. Don't take this to mean an actor shouldn't always have a monologue committed to memory just in case someone asks to see it.

A further reason to have a reel is in case you blow an audition. If the casting director really believes in your work, she can show your reel to the director and many times convince him to see you again. I dare say, almost every director has had his mind changed in this manner.

The best film on yourself to have would be from network television or a feature film. And if you have dialogue with a particular star, be sure to use that footage. But many actors and especially those just getting started don't have such film to show. Universities with strong film and television departments are sources where you can get good footage of yourself. The reason I say "strong" is because you don't want cheap-looking footage to show to agents, casting directors, and ultimately, directors. It would be better to have no film than "bad" film. Many universities have film festivals for their students' films, and industry people do attend. The American Film Institute, USC, and UCLA do the best work in this area in Los Angeles. I was an instructor at the American Film Institute in the eighties and I can attest that their work is top-notch.

Those who are not members of SAG or AFTRA can get good footage of themselves from non-SAG and non-AFTRA shows. These are shows that aren't shot under union jurisdiction, so they use people who usually haven't had an abundance of screen acting experience. (Non-union productions are discussed in more detail in Chapter Fourteen.)

Important point: Put a still shot (freeze-frame) of your headshot at the beginning of your reel. This will help make you identifiable as people watch your work. If your name isn't on your headshot, it should appear at the bottom of the screen during the freeze-frame of your headshot.

HAVE DIALOGUE on your demo reel. Industry people aren't interested in seeing you as a spear-shaker. In Los Angeles and New York, information about university productions is obtainable from the trade publications already discussed. Most of the college film production auditions in Los Angeles and New York are usually open to anyone who wishes to audition. That's because in those cities there is such a talent pool to select from and even professionals like to get better film on themselves than they might presently have.

In the smaller markets, simply phone local college film and TV departments to find out about their auditions. Some of the universities will allow student filmmakers to have open auditions; others will restrict the filmmakers to auditioning only registered students at their institution. Another option is to contact local film and video production companies and inquire about their productions. Many cities have companies that specialize in shooting educational and industrial films and tapes.

Of the many advantages to performing in student films, one of the long-term benefits is that you will probably work with some of those same people again in the future when they're no longer students. Many of the people I currently work with were classmates of mine at California State University. Who knows, the director of that student film you starred in might go on to direct feature films in the future.

If you are cast in any type of show, be sure to get a copy of your scene(s). You can have this done at just about any editing facility. Many of the film departments of the colleges where you were in a production have the facilities to do this for you. Check first that their equipment is top-notch and you will be obtaining as clean a copy as possible. By "clean," I mean that they haven't "generated it down" so many times that the quality will suffer and so will the look of your performance.

Keep in mind, your reel should be short; five minutes is long enough, perhaps too long! I sit with suits day after day looking at actors' demos, and it is extremely rare that anyone watches over a minute or two. This means put your best work first and have it edited in such a way that your scene(s) "cut" very quickly to show your talents in an extremely timely manner.

I know what you're thinking, "But Tom, I want my scenes to build to a climax...." Fine, but this is only a reel; no one will be watching your Academy Award–winning climax by the time your demo builds to it. We know enough about your acting within a very short period of time to make a decision on your abilities. Let's say you've scheduled a five-hour blind date. After you open the door, how long does it take you to decide whether this is going to be a good date or a bad date? If your answer is over five seconds, you're lonely.

It is possible that you might decide at dinner later that your initial impression about the date was incorrect. It's not like that for us when viewing an actor's reel, because we rarely get the chance for anything other than an initial impression.

With no other source for a reel, you could turn to a company, especially in Los Angeles, which for a fee will make you a demo. The companies that make demo reels for you will likely have the same effect on your career that daylight has on Dracula; their reels are a waste of time, but I guess there are exceptions. They usually look very amateurish and any professional viewing it wonders why you couldn't have gotten into some actual university film or TV production. Consider the agent's point of view: Why should an agent look at homemade demos of actors who obviously haven't worked in a professional or university production, when she can view demos of other actors in actual shooting situations?

If you have a demo reel, I repeat, it's a good idea to mention that on your resume and in your cover letter. Anytime you have an interview with anyone in this business, take your demo with you. Keep a copy of your reel in the trunk of your car, even if you aren't on your way to an audition. You never know who you're going to run into.

The drop-by method discussed with regard to your photo and resume can be used for your demo, also. Take it to various agents' offices, without an appointment. Some of them will accept your demo; others will tell you to get lost. Hey, it's worth a try! The advantage of the demo reel is that industry professionals can view it at their convenience.

Do not give anyone original footage! Demos almost always get lost in the shuffle and we don't have time to spend the afternoon at the post office mailing everyone's material back. You can send a self-addressed, stamped envelope with the hopes of receiving your material back. Most people do try to return material when it is sent in this manner, but there are no guarantees.

Hear me out on this one—it is vital! You must put your name, the name of your agent (if you have one), and contact numbers on the box the demo comes in, on the sleeve on the actual tape or DVD itself, and have them presented on your reel at the beginning and the end. And be sure to include your photo and resume with your reel. I can't stress how important this is!

Your goal here is to find a way to show the agents your abilities. No matter how talented you are, if they don't see your work the talent is useless. Few agents will take you on as a client without seeing some of your work first. If you're talented you want them to see your work. An agent will have more confidence in you if she knows what you can do, and if she likes what you can do she'll work harder for you.

An agent puts her reputation at stake every time she sends you to an audition; she'll be depending on your skills as an actor. If you do a poor job, then, unfortunately, it reflects badly on your agent.

YOU can get an agent. You will get an agent, but it might not be as soon as you are imagining. It wouldn't be unusual that you sent your package to every single agent in Los Angeles, for example, and didn't hear from any of them. You just tell yourself that you're going to continue to try and contact the agents even after they've turned you down time after time.

Every star has been turned down by some agent. In fact, every star has been turned down by many, many agents. And by the same token, agents are turning down many future stars at this very minute. Perhaps you're one of them. The important thing is that you need to keep your head up.

The odds will eventually be in your favor if you keep sending out your packages to the agents, continue trying to get some good film on yourself, and keep acting in plays/showcases around town and inviting agents to come see you perform. All the prep work you have done will pay off; you will obtain an interview with an agent. How to handle that interview, as well as other aspects of dealing with agents, will be discussed in the next chapter.

Managers

You've read all those stories about the managers of big stars, and you've seen those magazine photos of them standing together palling around. So you decide that if you just had a manager, you, too, could reach stardom and big money. Well, if you're just starting out I wouldn't suggest automatically going the manager route—you don't have a career to manage yet. But there are exceptions. You have to know what you're doing when it comes to picking a manager. And for this there are no unions to protect you.

Beginners should be very cautious when it comes to signing a contract with a manager. There are exceptions, of course. I personally know some excellent managers out there who can help you obtain agency representation and will work extremely hard for you. But you really have to do your homework. Here are a few pointers when dealing with managers:

- The manager's job is to manage your career. The manager will help you change agents when, or if, it becomes necessary. He will keep on top of your agent to make sure the agent is adequately representing you. The manager also solicits work for actors, much in the same way as an agent does. One advantage of a manager is that you'll have another person working on your behalf. Another advantage, assuming he's a good manager, is that a manager normally handles fewer people, around ten to twenty clients, whereas an agent may handle ten to twenty times that number.

- As with agents, any manager who charges you money up-front for representation isn't legit. Once you have a job, a manager usually takes around 15 percent of an actor's salary, but it could range from 10 to 20 percent. That's 15 percent on top of the agent's 10 percent. But if the manager helps you obtain work, your remaining 75 percent of something is better than 100 percent of nothing.

- Since managers aren't licensed agents they can't legally negotiate contracts with employers. In Los Angeles, for example, according to California State law in statute 1700.44(D), managers are allowed to negotiate contracts if they do it in *conjunction* with a licensed agent. They may also be able to do this through an attorney, but not by themselves. Some managers do negotiate directly, although they aren't supposed to. It happens because many managers have personal friends who are directors, producers, etc. Whether or not you have a manager, you still need an agent!

Some great managers, ones who have terrific connections, can do wonders for your career. Others can't do anything. If you are considering signing with a manager, I would suggest having as short a contract as possible, although you must allow them some time to build your career. This is understandable.

Some agents don't like working with managers, because in effect the managers are looking over their shoulders to see if they're working for you. Other agents enjoy working in conjunction with a manager to build an actor's career.

Once you've finally obtained an interview with an agent, how do you handle that interview? Read on.

Sample Photo/Resume Cover Letter to Agents

Bill Ray
1111 South Street
Anywhere, CA 00000
555-555-5555

(date)

Mr. Joe Smith
Joe Smith Agency
2000 Some Street
Hollywood, CA 00000

Dear Mr. Smith:

I am interested in representation with your agency. My most recent acting credit was with The Theatre in Miami. I played Fyedka in *Fiddler on the Roof.*

Thank you very much for taking the time to look over my enclosed photo and resume. I hope to hear from you soon.

Very cordially,
Bill Ray

Enclosure: headshot and resume

Sample Letter to Invite Agents to Showcase Plays/Workshops

Bill Ray
1111 South Street
Anywhere, CA 00000
555-555-5555

(date)

Mr. Joe Smith
Joe Smith Agency
2000 Some Street
Hollywood, CA 00000

Dear Mr. Smith:

I am inviting you to see me perform in *You're a Good Man, Charlie Brown*, being performed at the North Hollywood Little Theatre, located at 0000 Mission Road.

Please phone the theatre at 555-555-7777 to obtain your complimentary tickets. The play will run September 16 - 25. Curtain time is 8:30 P.M.

Enclosed is a flyer on the play, along with my headshot and resume. I am seeking representation, so I hope you will see me perform. Thank you for any consideration.

Very cordially,
Bill Ray

Enclosures: flyer on play
            headshot and resume

CHAPTER TWELVE

Do Come Prepared for Your Meeting with the Agent

You finally land an interview, after an extended period of time of trying to get into an agent's office. It is a very important step in your career, but not the end-all. Relax! This might be the first interview you will have with an agent, but believe me, if you stay in the business for any length of time it certainly won't be the last.

When does the actual interview begin? When you start your audition? No. When you walk into the actual agent's office? No. When you meet the secretary in the outer office? No. When you arrive in the parking lot? No. The interview begins when you're first informed that there's going to be a meeting with an agent, because there is prep work to be done, which I discuss in this chapter.

Even when you arrive in the parking lot, the interview is taking place. I've sat in auditions where the client didn't want a particular actor because "he cut me off to get that parking space." As ridiculous as it sounds, this has happened on more than one occasion. I've been in the men's restroom before an audition while an actor, who didn't know I was the director, was less than kind. For me, this probably wouldn't stop me from casting a particular actor, but there are many people who must like you before you will be cast. And a director is considering how each actor he casts will interact with the rest of the cast and the entire crew.

How to Dress

Dress casually for the interview. Men don't need to wear coats and ties, unless that's the type of characters for which you'll most likely be auditioning. Women don't need to wear high-fashion dresses. Wearing clothes that cost more money than it would take to feed the population of China is a no-no. And, as I said with regards to actual auditions, don't wear heavy makeup.

Back in the early days of film much of the acting was very stylized; everything from makeup to acting styles was exaggerated. The early film actors had come from the stage where everything is played much broader. Screen stars were glamorous. Compare that with the look of our stars today—most of today's are more natural looking.

Commercials in the eighties and early nineties were mainly hard sell. Since then, they are usually more natural with everyday-looking people.

I'm not saying you should dress like an unmade bed. If you look as though you could walk into a rummage sale and get sold, then you're probably underdressed. Select something in between as the best policy. Nice jeans/slacks and shirt for men are pretty standard. As with your photographs, you want to keep the attention on your face.

For women, you shouldn't wear clothes that look as though the seamstress ran out of material. Only consider dressing sexily for an interview if you think those are the kinds of roles you'll be auditioning for in the future, but even then, be subtle about it.

Be on Time

Be on time for the interview. Arriving late tells the agent that you are not a very responsible person and are not taking your career seriously. And if you're late to meet an agent, it gives the agent the idea you might be late for auditions for casting directors and directors, and that reflects badly on the agent. Punctuality is the agent's first impression of you. And first impressions stick. If you're meeting an agent in Los Angeles, take into account that traffic there is very unpredictable. That's before you reach the problem of parking! There's a name for the Los Angeles City Council's parking plan—

neglect. No matter in what city you're meeting an agent, leave for the interview much earlier than you think you should.

Being late causes you stress, as I said previously. You need to get to an audition early so that you can relax and compose yourself before your meeting.

What to Bring

Bring photos and resumes to the interview. Bring your headshot, plus the proof sheets from the original shooting from which you selected your headshot, if you have them. If you had a few 8 x 10s printed before you decided which one(s) you actually wanted to use for your headshot(s), bring them too. The extra photos will give the agent a better idea of how you photograph. (Note: It isn't mandatory to have the proof sheets and extra photos.)

Come with a couple of short monologues prepared if you're going to have an interview with a stage agent. One should be a serious monologue and the other a humorous one, each around three minutes or less in length. Most stage agents, however, would rather see you perform in a workshop or showcase. (Refer back to the discussion of showcase plays/workshops in Chapter Eleven.)

Even if you're going to have an interview with a screen agent, it's a good idea to prepare a short monologue, preferably something light and humorous, though few of them will actually want to see you perform one. It's better to be safe than sorry. If the screen agent wants you to bring in prepared material, he'll usually notify you in advance of the interview; he would most likely want you to bring in a two-person scene, because he's more concerned about how an actor reacts to, and plays off, another actor. If the agent does want you to perform a two-person scene you'd probably be expected to show up with another actor. And bring your demo reel if you have one!

An agent requesting that you bring in a two-person scene for the interview wants to see *you*, so pick one that will show *you* off rather than your partner. In most cases the scene, like the monologue for screen agents, should be light and humorous. Yes, Shakespeare is beautiful. I love Shakespeare. But let's be honest here. We're not doing *King Lear*; we're selling hamburgers for goodness sake. And Shakespeare's material isn't likely to give the screen agent much knowledge of how natural you are with dialogue.

Be mentally prepared for a "cold reading" if you're going to have an interview with a TV, film, or commercial agent. Giving a cold reading means that you'll be reading the material with little preparation, if any. The agent will give you some material to look over for a few minutes and then ask you to perform it. Unless the material is very short, most agents won't ask you to memorize it on the spot; hence the term, "cold reading"!

How you handle this cold reading is important because most roles for TV shows, films, and commercials are cast only a few days before the actual shooting. Roles for regulars in TV series (roles that appear on every episode) and the starring roles in films can take longer, but they, too, are sometimes cast within a few days of the actual shooting.

On numerous occasions, I have begun directing a feature film or a particular episode of a TV show even before all of the roles have been cast—sometimes casting the actors we need for the first few days of shooting and then casting the others as we get to them in the script. The director and/or writer may add characters as the shooting progresses. Scripts for the screen change daily.

In episodic TV we sometimes cast on the day between the shooting of each episode! In soap opera work, roles are cast as they crop up; the scripts are finalized only a few days ahead of each day's shooting. Commercials are cast and shot within a matter of days.

When I was an actor way back when telephone cords were kinky and the sex wasn't, I was usually cast the day before I would shoot a particular show and it always bothered me. I wondered why the director couldn't get his act together and cast a few days in advance, which would have given me more time to prepare. Now that I'm a director it has become clear to me why this happens. Feature film and television production is in constant flux—the only thing that remains constant is the flux.

Since time is money in TV and film, production people don't have time to send full scripts out to all the actors who will be auditioning for the show. Thus, almost all screen auditions will include a cold reading. It stands to reason, then, that a screen agent would want to know your cold reading capabilities before taking you on as a client. Sad to say, but basically you're cast for how good a cold reader you are rather than how great an actor you are. You'll find few people in the industry who will admit that, but it is the reality!

Conversely, you won't have to perform a cold reading for many stage agents if they don't handle actors for TV and film. Unless a play is original and being performed for the first time, it can usually be checked out of the library or obtained from Samuel French before an audition. So the stage actor usually knows most or all of the material in advance of an audition. Therefore, a cold reading is less used for stage interviews—but be mentally prepared for one anyway. For a stage agent, more than likely you'll be performing a monologue.

The Chitchat Session

Show the agent that you have a pleasing personality, such as we discussed earlier. Chat allows the agent to get a general feeling about you. If you're so nervous that you can keep coffee awake, you might find yourself giving either one- or two-word answers or going on and on saying nothing of any significance or interest. Try to catch your breath and avoid both extremes. The idea is to get the agent interested in you....so don't bore him! If the agent has seen better conversations in his alphabet soup, he probably won't be very impressed. After all, this is a personality business. Don't make it appear as though you went to the Cruella de Ville Charm School.

This chitchat session is more important than most actors think.

Agents are very aware that most directors have a good idea whether they want to hire a particular actor or not, even before the actor actually reads. A very small minority of directors don't even read the actors; they just feel out their personality and go with it. It's my belief that this isn't good director technique, but I've seen it done on more than a few occasions.

Establish some commonality of interest with the agent by a simple technique: Look around the interviewer's office and see what types of things he likes. A person's office often reflects his personality. Are there pictures of dogs on his walls? My office is full of my kids' photos. Since I'm a commercially rated pilot, I have photos of my airplane on the walls. Anyone who talks about family and airplanes has my attention.

At some point, the agent will probably ask you some variation on, "What have you been doing lately?" An answer such as, "About what?" isn't appropriate. Unlike your response to a director in an actual audition, your answer to an agent *should include* some of the things you've been working on towards your acting career. After all, that's where the agent's interest in you lies. But go further. He is getting an idea of your personality, so try and tell him some other interesting things. Keep the stories short, but you might tell him some funny episodes that have happened to you in your search for an agent, for example. Control yourself. You don't want an agent to have a hard time getting you out of his office.

If you don't have many credits, the agent might ask you with whom you are studying, or have studied, even though it should appear on your resume. If you're studying with someone in the same city as the agent, he might know something about your teacher. He might even have enough rapport with your teacher to phone him to see how you're doing. Occasions when I could go either way about casting a certain actor, I've been able to phone that teacher to get a better understanding how the actor works, because the chances of my knowing his acting teacher in Los Angeles or New York are good.

In talking to the agent, remember that who you're studying with won't carry nearly as much weight as having actual credits. Schooling is only a means to an end. I doubt any acting school will impress an agent as much as acting jobs. It's not college degrees that are important to them, but whether the actor received experience on the college stage. Would you rather hire someone who'd just finished contracting school to build a house, or someone who had actually built many homes?

If you have a heavy credit list, then the agent probably won't even ask with whom you've been studying. With few or no credits whatsoever, your answer to this question could take on real importance. And don't forget, it is a must that no matter how many credits an actor has he should constantly study acting.

During the interview, keep a positive attitude. The interview should be very "up." No agent wants to hear depressing stories about the hard time you're having getting started in the acting profession. Agents, as well as directors, producers, and casting directors are all struggling in this business. I'm sorry to say that we're not interested in your hard times. I don't mean to be cold, but let's face facts. If you were dating someone who kept telling you (verbally or otherwise) that no one else wanted him, you'd begin to realize why!

You should always send a very short thank-you note to the agent after the meeting. This is a must! Postcards with your photo printed on them are best because they remind the agent who you are. Don't write long letters that will most likely end up in a trash bin.

You will probably meet with many agents before one is interested in representing you. Eventually it will happen and you will end up with an agent who is willing to work with you. Your working relationship with that agent will probably be one of the single most important factors in your success, or lack thereof, in finding work in this industry. We'll discuss the actor-agent relationship next.

CHAPTER THIRTEEN

Do Have the Best Possible Working Relationship with Your Agent

An actor comes home from an audition one afternoon to find his best friend on his doorstep. The friend says to him, "You're not going to believe this, but your agent came by the house today and he stole your wife's jewelry, spent some time with her in the bedroom, and then they ran off together."

A moment later the actor asks, "My agent came by the house today?"

There is a perception in the heartland that an actor meets with his agent for lunch and they party together. And that's just what it is—a perception. Frankly, most agents don't know their clients very well at all. Numerous times I've been in a meeting with an agent, whose clients I was considering for a part, when the agent's intercom rang. The agent picks up the phone and hears the secretary say that so-and-so client is on the line, to which the agent responds, "Do I handle him?"

Agents handle a huge number of actors. A few years ago I was sitting in a top agent's office when a guy walked by the door very quickly. Because he passed by so quickly, the agent didn't get a good look at him.

Regardless, the agent stood up from behind her desk and yelled out, "I sent your photo to the studios, they're crazy about you." It turns out, she didn't even represent him. No one represented him. He wasn't an actor. He was the UPS guy.

In another instance, I was again in a top agent's office discussing the possibility of using one of his stars. After a few minutes this agent asked me if I wouldn't mind sitting over to the side of his desk while he interviewed an actor he had made an appointment with previously. Saying the actor was brand new, the agent commented that he would shoo her out the door as quickly as possible. I told him to definitely not shoo her out quickly, that I didn't mind waiting. Here was an actor who had probably been trying to get into an agent's office for years and I wasn't going to interfere with her chances of possibly picking up representation by this agent.

After talking to the actor for about five minutes the agent said, "You know, I have another actor who is the same physical type as you. Her name is Susan Keller and I can't even find work for her, so I have no interest in representing you."

Then he found out he already represented her! This actor was Susan Keller! The agent had been talking to one of his own clients and didn't even know it! She had come in to talk about her new photos and this agent had thought she wanted representation. These are by no means bizarre stories. They are somewhat typical.

Agency Contracts

Building a good, working relationship with your agent is much easier said than done. The first step would be to gain a clear understanding of how the relationship works legally. If an agent decides to represent you, he might want you to sign a contract on the spot or a few days later. I've stressed that you should sign a contract only with a union or union/association agent if you're in the major markets. Stick with that and you are basically protected from being ripped off.

The contracts you'll sign with a union agent are standard within each respective union. (There are some variations with union/association agents.) Ask to take the contracts home and read them over; there's nothing wrong with that. It makes good sense to read them over very carefully. Then you can contact the appropriate union or association to get reliable answers to any questions you might have.

When you sign contracts with a union agent, you'll sign three copies of each—one for the agent, one for you, and one for the appropriate union. It is an advantage for the union to have a copy because then they know who your representative is. Sometimes casting directors and directors phone the union to find out how they can get in touch with a certain actor. If you have signed contracts with an agent, the union will have that information for future employers.

The contracts you'll sign with a union or union/association agent guarantee that she'll make a percentage of your salary. The maximum a union agent can take from your salary is 10 percent, which is standard. (This is not necessarily the case with a union/association agent.) By the way, that's not 10 percent of your unemployment checks, although your agent could make the argument that she was responsible for them! (You may have heard of cases in which a star has negotiated a 5-percent take with an agent, but they are extremely rare.) Those of you working in a smaller market where there are no union or union/association agents will be paying a higher percentage—from 10 to 20 percent—which is somewhat standard outside of the major film and television markets.

It does happen that your employer will send your check(s) directly to you, but don't think your agent still won't know what you are being paid for each job. If she negotiated the contract, she'll obviously know what her and your cut should be. If you negotiated the contract yourself, all the agent has to do is check with the casting director for that particular show or contact the union to find out what you made on a particular job.

The union or union/association contract you sign with an agent states that no matter who gets you the job, and no matter who negotiates the contract, the agent is still entitled to her percentage. It is more common that check(s) will be mailed directly to your agent, on your written authorization. By the time you get your first job, your agent probably would've had you sign check authorizations; authorizations that give her permission to cash your checks from any acting employment. For union agents, the performer must authorize this and can rescind it at any time. (This is not necessarily the case with union/association agents.) When an agent receives your check from a production company, she'll deposit it into her bank in an escrow account or client trust account, and write you a check for your 90 percent of the original amount. Again, all this assumes you're dealing with union or union/association agents.

At this point, you might be wondering how you could protect yourself from being ripped off by your agent. Again, this is one of the main reasons you are dealing with union or union/association agents if you're in one of the major markets that have them. First of all, as is the case with your agent you'll know how much money you're making on the show, so you'll know what you and your agent's cut will be. Second, your agent will mail your statement of earnings from your employer with your check. Third, as stated earlier, the union has a record of how much you made on the job; you can phone its office if you have any problems. Fourth, you'll get your W-2 forms at the end of the year stating your earnings.

Quite frankly, I cannot imagine any union or union/association agent trying to rip you off. She would be putting her entire business at stake if she got caught doing such a thing; she could be punished and lose her license by, or affiliation to, the appropriate organization.

Escape Clauses

There are times when an agent wants to get out of a contract with an actor. One easy way is to stop submitting the actor for auditions and eventually the actor will move on to another agent. The union-affiliated actor who wants to release an agent, however, must adhere to certain provisions, as stated below. The same escape clauses apply no matter what the duration of the actor's contract happens to be. If you want to leave an agent and you fall into any of the situations listed, you simply send a registered letter to the agent informing her of your departure, keep a copy for yourself, and send a copy to the appropriate union or association.

For union agents (those working under traditional SAG agency rules): In regards to an initial film agency contract, if the actor fails to be employed (or be entitled to receive compensation) within the first 151 days of the contract, he can terminate the contract. Also, if there is no bona fide offer of employment within the first 120 days of that 151-day period, he can terminate the contract. If it is not the initial contract, the actor may terminate if he has not worked 10 days (or received compensation therefore) in the last 91 days. ("Bona fide offer" means that the agent has secured an actual acting job for the actor, contract and all, not just, for example, a submission of the actor's photo and resume.)

For SAG commercial contracts, if you haven't made $3,500 or more in commercials in a period of 151 days, you can terminate the contract. In other words, the same 151-day rule described for TV/film contracts applies here.

Your initial contract with any agent can only be signed for up to a maximum of one year. At the end of that time you can renew for a period of up to three years, if you're satisfied with the agent. If the agent is not satisfied with you, then you would not want him to represent you longer than that anyway. Any agent not excited about you, definitely won't put much effort into furthering your career.

For AFTRA franchised agencies: In regards to the Standard AFTRA Exclusive Agency Contract, if you have worked fewer than 10 days in the previous 91-day period, you are within your rights to terminate your agency contract. For the Standard AFTRA Commercial Exclusive Agency Contract, if you have not received the appropriate amount of compensation in the 91 days preceding the giving of notice of termination, you may terminate your agency contract.

For Equity franchised agencies: If you haven't had a bona fide offer of employment in the last 90 days, you can terminate the contract. The initial contract can be signed for a maximum of eighteen months. The second contract with the same agent can be signed up to a maximum of three years.

For ATA and NATR agencies: In the bylaws of both organizations it states that the agents have to abide by state law. In most cases, these agents insist that if an actor has worked one day in four months then the agent can hold the actor to that contract. However, ATA and NATR agencies may adopt their own individual contracts with their actor clients.

One Agent or More?

You can have different agents for different fields, even if you sign contracts with all of them. In other words, you can have a commercial agent, a TV/film agent, and a stage agent. Many agencies have a separate department for each field. If the same agent represents you for more than one area, you can release yourself from one of the areas if you're not happy with her in that particular area and retain her for the others. This can become touchy. You have to use your own judgment about whether to leave an agent for one field while retaining her for others.

It is against all union and union/association rules to sign a contract with more than one agent at the same time for a specific field in the same union local. In other words, you can't sign a theatrical contract or a stage contract with two agents in the same local. ("Theatrical" has nothing to do with theatre. As with "theatrical" photo, it refers to TV and film in this industry.) Under SAG, AFTRA, Equity, ATA, and NATR rules you can sign an exclusive contract with an agent for representation in New York and sign another with a Los Angeles agent for representation in Los Angeles for the same fields, because they are located in different union locals.

If you could sign with two agents for the same field in the same union local it would create a confusing situation for the casting directors, as well as present you with interesting legal questions. To whom would you pay your 10 percent, if you were signed with more than one agent for the same field? If you signed two contracts stating that you'll pay 10 percent to each agent and you get a job, you would now owe 20 percent, and it's against all union rules to pay more than 10 percent in agency fees.

On rare occasions at the beginning, you won't have to sign a contract with an agent who's working on your behalf. She might agree to work for you and wait until you obtain your first job before signing anything. SAG doesn't like this arrangement, but doesn't deter anyone from practicing it. And it's to your advantage to sign contracts with union or union/association agents; usually it means that the agent is more interested in you if she goes through the paperwork of signing you up. If she doesn't sign you right away, it doesn't necessarily mean she isn't interested in you, though.

Once you secure your first job the agent still doesn't have to sign contracts with you, though if she has not yet done so, this is most likely the time that she will. Even after you obtain employment and you haven't signed a contract, you are still obligated to give your agent her 10 percent for the life of the employment contract the agent negotiated. When you agree to work together, you have a verbal contract with that agent, and the unions and associations expect you to stand by that agreement. Be honest with your agent. Be a decent human being.

In Los Angeles, although again it isn't against SAG regulations, it would be extremely unwise to work under more than one agent for the same field even if you don't sign contracts. If you do, casting directors are confused about who your representative is and in the end you'll lose out; the casting director won't want to phone one agent to negotiate without talking to the other, because conflicts can occur. I remember times when I didn't call an actor in because two different agents submitted his headshot. I knew both agents personally and didn't want the hassle. In conclusion regarding Los Angeles: Don't have two agents representing you for the same field, even if no contracts have been signed.

In New York, on the other hand, it is pretty standard for an actor to work under different agencies even for the same field, without a signed contract. Then, whichever agent gets you in the door, gets the commission if you land the job. This applies *only* if you don't have a signed contract. In New York, casting directors and directors are aware that actors may be working under more than one agent for the same field and it doesn't seem to be a problem for them.

I pointed out earlier that some agents handle all areas, some a combination, and others only one area. Some actors prefer to have one agency represent them exclusively across the board, and some agencies insist on it. The advantage here is that all your business transactions will be going through one office. The disadvantage is that few agents, if any, are strong in all fields.

Taking into consideration that disadvantage, some actors choose to sign with an agency that specializes in the field of the actor's strongest interest, but has other departments as well. It happens, though, that many actors who are just starting out will end up with an agent who is a jack-of-all-trades—representing all areas, but not specializing in any particular one. In areas outside of the major shooting markets of Los Angeles and New York, it is common practice for agents to handle all fields because there simply isn't enough work to support them in only one area.

Shuffling agents can be tricky. Let's suppose you get signed by a terrific commercial agent. Then you start looking for a theatrical agent. Suppose you find a theatrical agent who also happens to represent actors commercially, but he wants you for both areas. Suppose further that this new agent isn't as good a commercial agent as the commercial agent you already have. What do you do? You want the theatrical agent, but you also want the terrific commercial agent.

There are no clear-cut answers. You'll just have to look at the situation from all angles and make your own decisions, should you end up with this problem. You'll find that most agents, if they really want you, will take you on as a client in only one area, without necessarily representing you in other areas, if this is your wish.

Actor/Agent Relationships

Yes, actors have egos, as do agents. Sometimes these egos clash. Actors always think they should be going out on more auditions than they are, and agents think actors should have more patience. So goes this business of agents for directors and producers also.

Actors and agents have a love-hate relationship. (The agent loves the actor; the actor hates the agent.) All kidding aside, actors sometimes talk badly about their agents—"The last audition I had was for *Gone with the Wind.*" "Last time I went on a film audition, they didn't have sound yet." Some comments like these could be warranted. I'll admit some agents and actors don't work well together, just as some psychiatrists and patients have problems. That first year is definitely a trial-and-error period for both of you. But, I'll repeat, don't badmouth your agent in auditions, or anywhere for that matter.

Be careful about sitting around talking about how bad luck has caught up with you with the agent you have. Thinking that karma is getting even with you because you played, "I'll show you mine, if you'll show me yours" with a former classmate in the third grade is destructive. Instead of complaining about your agent, simply call him up on the phone every once in awhile to ask if there's anything you can do to move your career along. Keep on your agent's back, but don't be a pest!

When you and your agent first decide to work together, it would be a good idea to ask her how often you should phone in. Some agents will tell you to phone in weekly. Others will tell you that if something comes up, they'll phone you. Whatever is decided, find a legitimate reason to phone your agent a few times a month, at the very least. It might be to inform her that you have just been cast in a play. Or perhaps to let her know you are taking a new acting class that you're excited about. It might be just to say you have been cast in a student film. This is better than just phoning to ask, "What's happening?" Even if you have nothing to promote, and you should always be working on that, phone your agent from time to time.

When you do phone, keep all conversations positive. Don't be negative. In this business no one likes whiners. Everyone in show business has his own problems, so be up with your conversations with your agent, or with anyone in this industry for that matter.

In the meantime, do a lot of hustling on your own. An agent has many careers to look after, and you have only one! What you do will not interfere with the work your agent is doing for you. Many actors will tell you that they get a lot of work on their own; even when they do they still need an agent for business reasons we've already discussed.

One of the things you can do is send photos and resumes to casting directors, and phone them to see if you can set up "general interviews" in which you just go into their offices and chat. A general interview isn't as important as an interview for a particular part. However, when your photo and resume are submitted to that casting director in the future, by you or by your agent, you may have a better chance of getting into the audition because the casting director has met you. You can obtain information about casting directors and their office addresses from many publications. Check with Samuel French bookstores in Los Angeles and New York, or Larry Edmunds Bookstore in Los Angeles, or The Drama Book Shop in New York for reference materials concerning the acting business.

Is Your Agent Working for You?

You may not realize that just because you aren't going out on auditions it doesn't necessarily mean your agent isn't working for you. Even if you have lots of credits and are a member of the acting unions, it's still hard for an agent to get you in the door to see casting directors and directors. Your agent isn't the only agent out there trying to accomplish this task.

There is a trick to finding out if your agent is submitting your photos and resumes. When you first go with an agent I wouldn't give her too many headshots and resumes. If you give her five hundred photos and resumes and within six months she hasn't asked for any more, that really doesn't clue you in on how much she has or hasn't been submitting you. Instead, give her far fewer, say fifty, and if after a year she tells you she has plenty of headshots and resumes left, you might want to rethink whether this agent is working for you. By giving her fewer photos and resumes you will need to have more frequent contact with her concerning her need for new headshots and resumes, assuming she is submitting them. However, you should always make sure she has plenty of photos and resumes. Never let your agent run out of them!

Let me point out that few actors obtain work in the first few months after signing a contract with an agent. Try and stick it out with your agent for awhile before releasing her from the contract. In the course of one year if you haven't gone out on a few auditions each month, then you can re-evaluate. Base your decision on whether to stick with that agent on how many auditions she's gotten you into during one year.

There are really no guidelines or statistics against which to judge how many times you should go out on auditions in the course of a year. I can tell you this: You will be sent out on them much less than you think you should. Once obtaining an agent, you might not be sent out at all. Check with other actors who are your physical type to see how much they've been going out, although just because they might be going out more than you doesn't necessarily mean you should be going out as much. What about their credit lists? Have they been in the business longer than you? Do they have some special ability that you don't have? Consider all the possibilities before condemning your agent—then condemn her!

Are you contributing to your career, or are you sitting around expecting your agent to do all the work? Agents can't build your career by themselves. You are supposed to have a partnership. Agents expect you to do some hustling on your own, especially when you're just starting out.

Your agent can't be as excited about your career as you are—no one will be! And again, we're all on the same boat—the Titanic—on this one. Directors obtain most of their directing jobs on their own. Most producers get their own jobs! So, don't feel as though you're alone on this one.

There are so many things you can be doing on your own. I've mentioned the SAG Conservatory, if you're a member of SAG, or are under age fifteen. And industry-night workshops, showcase plays, and so forth. You can send your package to casting directors. After submitting them, it's extremely rare that you will hear from any. Extremely rare! However, you never know. Keep at it and eventually some will respond. Once in a blue moon it happens that your photo lands on a casting director's desk at the exact moment that casting director is casting a part for which you're perfect. Admittedly, it's a long shot. But your packages have no chance of obtaining work for you by sitting in your residence. So start getting them out to people!

Leaving an Agent

Fitting an actor with an agent is about as difficult as fitting someone with shoes. The agent that was so right for you at the beginning of your career—the one who loyally sat through all your plays—might not be the right agent for you as your career grows. For the agent who worked so hard for you, this is sad. However, this is a business and agents understand this unfortunate situation.

If you realize that your agent represents the Unknown Soldier and that she can do nothing more for your career, don't break off relations immediately. Find another agent first. Start sending your photos and resumes to other agents and see what responses you receive. Don't worry too much about one of these prospective new agents phoning your current agent to tell her you are looking for other representation. It's basically not done and would be a rare instance if it did happen. In the slight chance that it did happen, it could be to your benefit if your original agent still wants to work for you. It might prompt her to work a little harder on your behalf.

Always be nice to your old agent. Don't give her a piece of your mind. There are too many times when actors end up coming back to an agent they've had before. You should make no enemies in this business. You might even send the old agent a postcard on her birthday, or whatever, just to keep in touch. You never know. The agent you were rude to might become a producer some day.

When you interview with a new agent, do not put down the old one! I can't stress this enough. Putting anyone down in any situation is a no-no in this business, as I emphasized in Chapter Five. It might lead the new agent to worry that you're going to do the same thing when you leave her. It's bad business. The acting community is a very small one.

The reason I say that when you start looking for another agent you shouldn't drop your old one first is that you might find that no other agent wants to take you on as a client at the moment. In that case you would still have your old agent to represent you. If I haven't already convinced you that having an agent is crucial to the development of your acting career, then you will be after you read the next chapter.

CHAPTER FOURTEEN

Do Understand the Entire Casting Process

How many actors does it take to screw in a light bulb? Three—one to screw it in and two to say, "I could've done that better." Every actor thinks he's the best person for the job. And every actor should believe this. Yet, the reality is, there's only one person who will be cast per role. And how that role is cast is kind of a complicated process.

If you want to do stage work, then New York is where the main action is. If you want to do TV and film work, then you should "Go west, young man." Commercials are cast on both coasts, although Los Angeles leads in this area. This is not to say that there's no TV and film work in New York, or no stage work in Los Angeles, but New York is a theatre town and Los Angeles is a screen town. Be clear on this, because when I write about the screen world, the slant will be towards Los Angeles, and when I write about the theatre world, the slant will be towards New York. However, the principles in their respective fields are about the same on both coasts.

TV and Film

You open your local newspaper in Omaha and notice that a local theatre is casting a play entitled, *Teen Sluts from Hell.* After reading a description of the characters, you decide you're right for the male role of the girls' gym coach. So you stroll on down to the theatre to read for the part. The competition is stiff, as there are thirty other perverts who are also right for the part. It all seems easy enough, because the theatre is having open auditions and you'll at least get seen.

You got the part and your performance in the play was terrific. You mastered the play at the local level and Auntie Susan urges you to go for the big time. The local papers gave you rave reviews, so you must be professional material.

You move to Los Angeles or New York, but when you open the daily newspapers there you don't see any auditions for acting roles. (I'd be skeptical of any auditions I read about in mainstream newspapers in Los Angeles or New York, anyway.) This is very frustrating. Here you are in the big city and you're ready to go, but you don't know where to go to!

At this point, you find out about some SAG and AFTRA (and non-union) shows, which are being cast, from *Backstage West* in Los Angeles and *Backstage* in New York. In addition to these publications, in New York you can look through *Variety* (weekly), and in Los Angeles in *Variety* (daily) and the *Hollywood Reporter* (daily). In Los Angeles, *Variety* and the *Hollywood Reporter* list production news only once a week, so check with their offices to find out which days.

Non-Union Productions

Non-union productions are often cast from actors who find out about auditions from the publications cited above. In most cases, actors can get into non-union production auditions without the aid of an agent.

Should you bother to audition for non–SAG and non–AFTRA jobs? Before deciding consider the following points: Non–SAG and non–AFTRA mean that the company shooting the show isn't a signatory of the respective union. If you're in one of these productions, should the company go bankrupt, or have some creative bookkeeping practices, you might never see your check. Whereas, with a union production, if the company doesn't have a long-standing record of good payment with the union, or if it is a new company, it has to post a bond (that is, money) to cover the actors' salaries, *before* using the actors.

Further points are that not very many industry people see these low-budget, non-union productions. There are exceptions. But what is your interest in performing in one? It really isn't the exposure or the money, but rather to obtain the film on yourself. You won't have the competition of union actors with non-union productions since union actors are forbidden from working in these shows.

Union and union/association agents may solicit non-union work for their non-union actors, though in Los Angeles and New York they rarely do so. In the smaller markets, this would be a more common practice. In Los Angeles and New York the main reason a union or union/association agent would get involved in non-union work for a non-union client would be for the same reason you would—to get good film on the actor. Union and union/association agents may still sign contracts with a non-union actor, whether the agent is getting the actor union or non-union work.

If you aren't a member of the screen unions, then you really have nothing to lose by participating in a non-union production as long as you are extremely careful about any contracts you sign. The contracts for employment with non-signatory companies don't tend to be standard, so have an entertainment attorney look them over carefully.

Union Productions

Though you can find out about some union auditions from the trade publications, roles for union TV and film auditions are cast almost exclusively through agents. Finding out about a union audition and getting yourself into that audition are two totally different things!

When a role is to be cast, the casting director will usually call Breakdown Services, a publication and online service with offices and editions in Los Angeles, New York, Vancouver, Toronto, and London. He will give Breakdown Services the vital information about the casting: how to get in touch with the casting director, the director's name, the producer's name, the dates the project is going to shoot, a description of the characters, and more. (You'll find a sample copy of an actual Breakdown casting page at the end of this chapter.)

Breakdown saves everyone time and money. Agents don't have time to read every script being shot in their area. In fact, they rarely have time to read any. And besides, as a director I'm not really interested in sending a complete script to every agent and manager, because not only is it costly and time-consuming, there's also a privacy issue here. We might be trying to get the jump on another studio with a particular story.

Breakdown Services distributes the information they are given to union and union/association agents and managers on a daily basis. Actors cannot obtain it directly. We consider this information confidential. Hollywood is a strange place, isn't it? It seems odd that the very people who need the information about where the jobs are can't obtain that information!

Breakdown Services does, however, provide some free casting information to actors. A casting director might want the information for a particular character put out to everyone so, through Breakdown Services, they use an online service called "Actor's Access." Just go to www.breakdownservices.com and click on "Actor's Access." In comparison to the list agents and managers receive, this listing is very small. This is one of the many reasons why you need an agent to represent you. (By the way, Breakdown Services has many publications and services for actors, including an online store. Visit their website for information.)

Each agent submits (by mail, in person, or online) actors' photos and resumes to the casting director. You should know that generally casting directors aren't looking for "new" people. It's a misconception to believe otherwise, no matter what you've heard. Each time a casting director sends an actor to a director he is putting his reputation on the line. The casting director's job is to find good, qualified people to send to the director. Therefore, they naturally feel much more comfortable working with actors who have proven themselves and/or who they've worked with in the past. Agents are mindful of this as they submit photos and resumes to casting directors.

In addition, agents like to submit actors who are physically right for the part, who have some decent credits, and who have a chance of getting into the audition. In Los Angeles there are roughly 600 agencies (not *agents*, but *agencies*), some of whom have dozens of agents in them; fewer in the smaller cities, of course. If each L.A. agency submitted only ten actors for a particular role, that would be about 6,000 actors up for the role even before the audition begins! Matters get worse, because most agencies wouldn't submit only ten actors.

Also, besides the ones submitted by agents, other actors will be trying to get into the audition. There will be those trying to get in on the side because they already know the casting director, director, or producer, or they heard about the audition on their own and sent their photo and resume to the casting director independently. Compounding the number, there will be managers submitting their clients. (There will be some overlap here because those actors probably also have agents submitting them.) Nevertheless, the director will want to see actors with whom he has worked before, as will the producer(s), writer(s), and others.

Now the casting director sorts through all of these photos and resumes and selects maybe several hundred to be interviewed for the pre-read (e.g., the meeting you have with the casting director before auditioning for the director). The number of actors seen for the pre-read varies widely. Some directors, myself included, like to give as many actors as possible a chance at auditioning for each role. Other directors will want the number limited. The numbers may vary, but the casting process is the same.

Your chances of getting in on that audition might be helped if the casting director is a personal friend of your agent. The opposite would be the case if your agent used to date the casting director and they broke off on sour terms; your chances of getting in would be damaged. This can all sound pretty petty, right? Welcome to big-time TV and film. Not only do these things happen, they happen on a daily basis. If you think they don't, then you should consider enrolling in that Reality 101 course being taught at the local college.

With those selected actors, the casting director sets up general interviews. (Note: As previously mentioned, on all auditions bring along a photo and resume, even though copies will most likely have been submitted earlier by your agent.) Since the casting director is calling people into the audition after viewing their photos, you can see why it's important that your photos accurately represent you.

The casting director's interview with these actors will be somewhat like the interview with an agent; you will be asked some of the same types of questions. Like the agent, the casting director is trying to get an idea of your personality and type. He may or may not have you read on this first meeting; it depends on how much time he has to cast the show. With very little time to cast this show, if he doesn't ask you to read, then he might not be interested in you physically for this part and needs to move on with the casting. However, don't take anything that happens in an interview as good or bad. As I've discussed with regards to auditioning, you really have no idea what the casting director is thinking, because many times he doesn't know himself.

After interviewing these actors, the casting director will probably call back around a hundred. Expect less for sitcoms, since he has less time to cast them than other types of shows. The casting director contacts the agents of those hundred or so actors to inform them when the callbacks will be held.

Let's say you're one of the lucky few to be called back. On this callback you'll probably see the script and give a cold reading of the material, during which the casting director will be looking to see how believable and natural you can be in your reading.

The casting director is just looking for good plain ol' conversation. He doesn't want actors to *read* to each other; he wants actors to *talk* to each other. Unfortunately, many newcomers to TV and film who are used to working only on the stage, don't realize that TV and film acting is much more subtle. In the screen medium "less is more" (possible exceptions: some commercial acting, and, in many cases, sitcoms filmed in front of live audiences). But none of the acting, even in these mediums, is as "big" as stage acting.

Most likely the casting director will shoot this audition. Sometimes the casting director will not read entire speeches that come inbetween your lines, but will jump right to the cue line for your speeches. My feeling is this is a real disservice to the actor because, you and I know, it's the reactions that "tell" the scene. You can understand why they do this; they have a lot of actors to audition and don't want to waste time. For my casting sessions, I ask the casting director not to do this.

Another way the casting director tries to move things along is to read at a faster pace than an actor normally would. This tends to make the actor start reading faster, although it doesn't mean that you have to keep pace. Most actors who are auditioning for TV and film roles are apt to rush their scenes. Think back to that speech you had to give in high school that was supposed to be five minutes in length. You practiced at home and your speech came out to five minutes, ten seconds. Your next rehearsal it came out to five minutes, fifteen seconds. The third brought it in at five minutes, eight seconds. Then you got up in front of the class and you were done in one-minute-and-a-half! You got nervous and speeded things up. The exact same thing happens to actors in auditions.

If the casting is for a feature film, then the recorded auditions will usually be sent to the director for viewing. For a TV show, they will be sent to a committee (producers, director, writers, and others), though if the committee is in a hurry, they may attend the audition and no recording would be made. If recorded, auditions for a commercial will be sent to the director and the account executives at the ad agency. The director will view the playbacks and decide who he wants to meet. The casting director might make some suggestions of his own, but the director and/or producer generally make the final decisions on whom to meet at this callback. Directors do at least listen to what the casting director suggests, since casting directors know the talent pool much better than they do.

Casting directors can be very helpful to the director at this stage of the audition. Maybe an actor didn't read very well, but I love his look; I can turn to the casting director who might have prior knowledge of the actor's capabilities. The casting director might have seen a particular actor in a film and suggest I watch that film, since his audition wasn't that terrific. It has happened to me on many occasions and I've ended up seeing the actor again. I've even ended up casting actors based on some other project and not their audition for us. Depending on the director/casting director's relationship, some directors will leave it to the casting director to decide who's going to meet the director.

So, the director likes you and your acting and calls you in for another reading. At this meeting the producer and/or suits may be present with the director. For a TV show, you might have to be sent to the network for "Network Approval." However, with the possible exception of a few of the regular roles on a series, the director and/or producer usually have final say over the casting of their show.

Earlier I said that casting directors don't cast and don't direct. There is one exception to this: Often in soap opera work, the casting director will cast the "Under Fives." These are roles that have fewer than five lines, under the jurisdiction of AFTRA. They aren't principal roles and they aren't extra roles either. It's an in-between category that taped television shows use. SAG and Equity have no such category.

I highly recommend that beginning actors try to obtain some Under Fives. Many times the person who casts these parts doesn't cast the other speaking roles. While he may also cast the extras, another casting director probably casts the principal parts. The advantage for an actor here is that the extras' casting director is sometimes easier to contact than the casting director responsible for the larger speaking roles.

Reminder: Doing Under Fives fulfills the eligibility requirement for working under the jurisdiction of a 4A union for joining SAG. Of course, you will still have to be a member of AFTRA for a year before joining SAG if you want to get into SAG through AFTRA, but at least you have an "insurance policy" that you will eventually be able to join SAG.

If you're in Los Angeles or New York, simply find out which soaps are shot in your city. Then contact the production company that shoots the show and ask who casts the Under Fives. Next, submit your photo and resume to that person. The process of obtaining these types of roles isn't easy, because they frequently go to actors who auditioned for larger roles but weren't cast. Other times they are given as favors to certain agents and friends of certain people. Be that as it may, this is a great place to start building a resume. When I first moved to Los Angeles to work as an actor, one of my first acting jobs was an Under Five on *General Hospital*. That led to a "recurring" role on the same soap that lasted for over twelve years. You can't expect that to happen, but the point is this is a good place to try and start one's career.

Usually, the entire casting process takes place over the span of a few days to a week or so; for film roles it is somewhat longer. (If we keep you on the interview for over an hour, or specifically ask you to take the script home and learn a scene, you might be entitled to compensation, provided it's for a union job and you're a member of the union. Check the union offices for information about any specific instances.)

By now it should be obvious that many people have to like you and your talents before you are cast in a TV show or film. Everyone's job rests on you, the actor. If your performance is lacking, guess who is going to get blamed? The director! So, unlike the suits and others who might be ill-informed about what makes a good actor, the director has more concern than just about everyone else. I am responsible for giving the suits a return on their hard-earned dollar. That is one of my primary goals as a director. I'm going to make sure that the acting is top-notch, although I might have to stand my ground and fight for the actors who will best serve the project.

The idea that you can fool around with a couple of people in the entertainment industry and make a career is hogwash. Just because your legs stay open longer than IHOP doesn't mean you will be hired. Too much money and too many careers and reputations are at stake when you're hired to do an acting job for most of us to practice such nonsense.

Theatre

It should be clear that, just as with TV and film, the casting of roles for theatre is important. Huge sums of money are invested in stage shows and one actor not working out could possibly mean the closing of a show long before the break-even point.

Concerning professional theatre acting over screen acting, there's good news and bad news. The good news is, it's easier for an actor to get seen by theatre producers than for their screen counterparts. Unfortunately, the good news causes the bad news: Since it's easier to get seen there might be more people in competition for each part. Your most important consideration in being cast is first being seen.

Work in non-Equity community theatres to get good experience. This is where stage has one advantage over the screen for the actor. Because of the expense, it's much harder to practice working on the screen in actual productions, whereas small theatre groups spring up in just about every town.

If you're starting out in the theatre, any work is probably positive! Any experience is good, be it local or professional, though as I discussed earlier, nonprofessional productions on your resume carry much less weight than professional jobs. Eventually, you'll want to perform in Equity productions because this is where actors get paid. And since you're reading this book, I take it for granted that you want to ACT AND EAT AT THE SAME TIME.

To be seen by theatre directors, you don't necessarily have to have an agent if you're a member of Equity, though I would highly recommend one anyway. If you have an agent, generally, you'll have a more personal audition. Without an agent, you'll probably be herded in with the rest of the group and the audition will be somewhat like going through an assembly line. Theatre producers/directors see so many people in such a short period of time that it's harder for them to remember you than if you'd had a semi-private audition.

Look in the trade publications, already discussed, to read about theatre casting news. These trade publications list Equity and non-Equity production casting news. You can also check the bulletin boards at any of the Equity offices, plus visit their websites and phone their hotlines. Even non-Equity members may phone any Equity office for general information about Equity.

Types of Equity Productions

Equity has different types of productions for which you can audition; the variations are too numerous (and confusing) to cite here. I'll introduce the major, basic types. The basic Production Contract is used for theatres having only a single production; not a run of plays back-to-back. This type of contract has the highest wage minimums for actors. To relieve theatres of the high cost of the Production Contract, there are other types of contracts, which have lower wage minimums.

The requirements for a theatre being able to obtain lower minimums depends on several factors—size of the theatre, number of shows the theatre is performing back-to-back, number of players being used from one production to the next, etc. Many of the theatres under Equity contracts, other than the Production Contract, are affiliated with specific organizations.

These organizations negotiate contracts with Equity on behalf of the theatres that are affiliated with them. A partial listing of organizations and/or contracts follows:

LORT (League of Resident Theatres)—the negotiating body for Equity resident theatres all over the country. To be considered a resident company the theatre must be producing a series of plays; in other words, the theatre must not be set up to produce only a single production. LORT theatres are nonprofit organizations.

CORST & COST (Council of Resident Stock Theatres & Council of Stock Theatres—non-resident—respectively)—the negotiating bodies for dramatic stock companies all over the country. By Equity definition, to be considered a stock company the theatre must be producing two or more plays simultaneously. Stock companies are usually not nonprofit organizations, as are LORT theatres. The main difference between CORST and COST is that the former maintains a nucleus of performers from one play to the next.

TYA (Theatre for Young Audiences)—the contract used for plays being produced for children. By Equity definition, in order for a company to use the TYA contracts, usually the play must be performed in the daylight hours and cannot be over an hour-and-a-half in length.

CAT, HAT/BAT, OFF-BROADWAY, & WCLO (Chicago Area Theatre, Hollywood Area Theatre/Bay Area Theatre, Off-Broadway theatres, and Western Civic Light Opera, respectively)—the contracts used for the small geographical areas they include. The low wage minimums for the actors is generally because the houses are small. Actors can end up making more money under these contracts than they would under other Equity contracts because they can receive not only a base salary, but also a bonus, which is directly connected to the gross at the box office.

DISNEY WORLD/ORLANDO—the contract for performers at Disney World in Orlando, Florida.

SPTC (Small Professional Theatre Contract)—used for theatres with a seating capacity of 349 or less in cities located outside of New York, San Francisco, and the county of Los Angeles.

LOA (Letter of Agreement)—contracts for developing theatres. In these cases, Equity has a separate agreement with each individual theatre based on the particular situation of that theatre. There is no standard contract here. Pay scales differ for each situation.

When you are reading casting information about the above types of theatres, the contracts to be used will be referred to as Production Contract, LORT, CORST, COST, TYA, CAT, HAT/BAT, OFF-BROADWAY, WCLO, DISNEY WORLD/ORLANDO, SPTC, and LOA.

Equity Principal Auditions

All of the Equity theatres are required to have a certain number of "Equity Principal Auditions," which are open to all Equity members. Then, if time allows, they may see non-Equity members as well. These auditions are usually held two or three times a year, but the number varies from one Equity contract to another.

Because these are general auditions, it could mean the company may or may not be seeing people for specific roles. As an example, to fulfill his theatre's obligation for the Equity Principal Audition, a theatre producer from Miami might travel to New York twice a year to interview actors for his entire production schedule for that year. However, many of the production companies consider the Equity Principal Audition a formality.

It does happen that some roles are actually cast from these principal auditions, although it is more usual for many roles to be cast through agents. Of course there are exceptions. The advantage for an actor to be seen at the Equity Principal Audition is that you might be kept in mind for future projects.

To give Equity credit, for its members the main advantage of the Equity Principal Audition is that they can be seen, whereas members of SAG and/or AFTRA have no guarantees of any screen auditions. For theatre, the basic elimination process for casting (callbacks, etc.) is handled somewhat the same as for TV and film roles. Stage actors may not have to go through as many people to get cast in a theatre role as screen actors—networks, sponsors, committees, etc. But this is not to say that it is easier to get cast in a theatre role than a screen role once you're able to get into the audition.

Most of the Equity Principal Auditions are held in New York and/or Los Angeles, even if the theatre is located in another city (exception: BAT and CAT auditions are usually held in San Francisco and Chicago, respectively). The reason being that so much of the Equity membership locates in New York and Los Angeles, theatre producers can audition from a larger pool of talent. Theatre producers are required to hold some of their auditions in any city where there is an Equity office. Each contract has its own rules for auditions. For example, LORT lists thirteen cities in which Equity Principal Auditions may be held, other than New York City, Chicago, and Los Angeles.

Understand that despite these requirements, it is uncommon for an Equity theatre to cast local talent for major roles. It depends solely on the theatre and the city where it is located whether they are open to casting local talent for these roles or not. But if there are Equity theatres near you and you want to become a professional actor, I urge you to try and get into their auditions, even if you're non-union. There's always a chance that they might see someone they really like, and keep that person in mind for the future. Let these theatres know who you are.

Sometimes Equity theatres will cast a very minor role locally, because it makes for good publicity to have a hometown local star working with the professionals. Under the various Equity contracts, Equity theatres are permitted to hire a nonprofessional or two to cast in their productions. It might be 10:1—for every ten roles to be cast, then under some Equity contracts, the producers could hire one non-professional. (See the Equity Membership Candidate (EMC) Program information in Appendix G.) Even though these nonprofessionals are sometimes cast during the principal auditions in New York and/or Los Angeles, at other times a local actor may be able to "break in." (Sounds like a criminal act!)

Food for Thought

Whichever medium you pursue, you'll go on many auditions from which you won't get cast. After every "no" to your face, you'll begin to wonder if you "have it or not," whatever that means. I've explained that the "no" generally has nothing to do with whether you "have it or not." It simply means you weren't right for that particular part and that particular part only. Even if this isn't the case, although it usually is, actors have to believe this or they run the risk of catching an acute case of the "actor's routine," and/or falling prey to the Beverly Theory.

Go back and review the first eight chapters, after you've been on a few auditions. You will look at those chapters in a different light and they will start to hit home with you.

Of course, you should always give the best audition you possibly can, but if you do happen to give a bad audition, and everyone does many times in their pursuit of roles, it won't be the end of your career. For some parts, you'll be too tall, too short for others; for some parts, you'll be too big, and too small for others. And so it goes.

You're bound to come home from auditions thinking, "If I had just read this line a little better," or "If I had put in that extra facial expression," (now you're doing the "actor's routine"), that you might have received the part. Forget it. The actor who did get the role might not necessarily have given the best reading. The odds are he didn't! He probably got the part for a number of reasons—he matched physically with the rest of the cast, he read decently, and the director probably liked his personality.

Sometimes you will hear about a part you're perfect for, but you won't even be able to get in on that particular audition, in spite of having a good agent. You have to accept that you won't get in on every audition you want to. Yes, it can be very frustrating. No one in this business will argue with you on that. Frustration is a part of this business.

We directors also hear about projects that we think we're perfect to direct and we can't get in to see the right people. After all, there's only one director on a film, but many actors, so you can see our job is hard, too. It should give the actor some comfort to realize that everyone in this business is struggling just as hard as he is, yet he tends to believe that it's just him who is struggling. It isn't the case. You have plenty of company when it comes to frustration with this business.

Since I give lectures and seminars worldwide, actors are constantly asking me if they have what it takes to make it as an actor. Guess what? I don't know. Anyone who tells you that you will or won't make it in this industry is either much more intelligent and perceptive than me, or much more naive. I'll take the latter.

I've had people come into auditions who I thought were going to be big stars and would have bet the family farm on. And where are they now? They are still working in the film industry—at Photo-Mat Drive-ins. Other actors who came in, I wondered who they were "dating" to get into this audition. Quite a few of those now have their own TV series and are major stars in motion pictures. Only you can decide whether you have what it takes or not. You are in a much better position to make that determination than we are. It all comes down to you believing in yourself as you go on audition after audition with few, if any, results.

While you're making the rounds and auditioning, you might want to eat! Isn't that what this book is all about? Unless you're blessed with an incredible inheritance, this means you need to work. If this is the case, seriously consider trying to get into the commercial acting field—my next topic.

Sample Breakdown Services' Casting Notice

BREAKDOWN SERVICES, LTD.
Los Angeles (213) 276-9166 New York (212) 869-2009 Vancouver (604) 488-6444 London (01) 488-2701
www.breakdownservices.com   The Link: www.submitlink.com

The information contained in this document is the exclusive property of Breakdown Services, Ltd. Any unauthorized reproduction, duplication, copying or use of the information contained herein, without prior written consent of Breakdown Services, Ltd., is strictly prohibited.

(File 0108f02-ljm) L
MARCIA SILEN FILMS
BLOODHOUNDS INC.
"FANGS FOR THE MEMORIES"
CHILDREN'S DIRECT TO VIDEO SERIES
(SAG OR AFTRA SCALE--
FALLS UNDER TV CONTRACT)

DEL'D IN LA Fri., Jan. 7, 2000, Vol. 2000, #0107
Casting Director/Line Producer: Olivia Perches
Director: Tom Logan
Interviews: January 18 & 19
Callbacks: February 1
Shoot Dates: February 15-February 19

WRITTEN SUBMISSIONS ASAP BY WED.,
2/13/00 TO:

OLIVIA PERCHES, CASTING DIRECTOR
TRI-P

AGENTS PLEASE DO NOT CALL UNLESS IT'S URGENT.
DROP SUBMISSIONS OVER GATE.

Directions: Go west on Washington Blvd. past Lincoln Blvd. 3 lights to Mildred, turn Right in a residential neighborhood.

PLEASE SUBMIT ASAP.
SUBMIT ALL ETHNICITIES FOR ALL CHARACTERS.

GUEST SPOTS--ALL OF THESE ROLES ARE STRONG ACTING ROLES. THIS DIRECTOR EMPHASIZES THE IMPORTANCE OF STRONG ACTING ABILITY.

[POLICEMAN] Male, age 40-60, but other ages considered if very character-oriented. Must be humorous. COMEDY A MUST...

[BRUCE] Male. Age 40-60. An appliance repairman. Overweight and the type who would wear his pants down around the middle of his behind. (Please don't do this on the audition.) VERY HUMOROUS. PLEASE DON'T SEND ANYONE WITHOUT VERY STRONG COMEDY BACKGROUND...

[MR. O'RILEY] An old man. Age 70+, the older the better. VERY STRANGE-LOOKING. Creepy-looking would be a plus. Very off-beat. He scares kids. COMEDY A MUST!...

[ANNA] Female. Age 30-50. An Elvira type. Very strange and weird. Very mysterious. MUST HAVE A MAJOR FLAIR FOR COMEDY...

[MORTIMAR] Male, age 30-60. Anna's sidekick. Very bizarre man from Transylvania. Could be tall and ball-headed, but other types considered. Perhaps bushy eyebrows. He should be very scary-looking. Maybe even a scar. Kids would run from this guy. Underneath, however, he's fuzzy...

[CHIEF OF POLICE] Male, overweight, very character-oriented. Should have a very interesting flair about him. COMEDY A MUST!...

[DOMESTICUS FOUR] A very strange robot. LOTS OF DIALOGUE, so voice extremely important. Voice should be very different and off-beat...COULD BE VOICE-OVER ONLY.

STORY LINE: Two kids, brother and sister have a detective agency. Every episode has them solving a crime and learning a moral lesson. Dad is played by Richard Thomas. Lots of stunts, location and sound work etc....

CHAPTER FIFTEEN

Do Pursue Acting in Commercials

The public thinks of television as a bunch of shows interspersed with commercials. We, however, think of television as a bunch of commercials interspersed with TV shows. Our reason being, commercials are very lucrative for everyone involved and they pay our salaries!

I know that many of your acting teachers pooh-pooh actors who do commercials. As you are "crawling around on the floor acting like a lion" and doing mirror exercises, many acting teachers lecture about the true art of acting. You know what? It all sounds beautiful. Don't get me wrong. I think all of this artsy stuff is wonderful. But you must eat!

Most actors underestimate what a commercial can do for them financially—or even that it comes under the category of acting. Being in a commercial may be one of the toughest acting jobs that you'll ever have. You have to create a likable character, deliver dialogue you wouldn't normally say (How many times have you heard two women running down the beach talking about how terrific their feminine deodorant is?), all in thirty to sixty seconds. It's much more difficult than it seems.

We've all heard newcomers in the acting business talk about doing some commercials to tide them over until they can do some real acting. You are acting when you're in a commercial! In my seminars, someone always asks something along the lines of, "Tom, do you think it would be harmful to my career if, when I first get out to Los Angeles, I did some small speaking parts on network shows and a few national commercials?" This question shows how little these actors understand about the commercial acting profession, and know about the industry in general.

If you get cast in a commercial, local or otherwise, have copies made; the same as with any film that you obtain of yourself. For those of you living in a small town, which doesn't have union or union/association agents, you can find out about local commercials from TV stations and from advertising agencies. (Note: Many regional commercials, and some local ones, are cast in the big two cities—Los Angeles and New York.)

The Bucks

Commercial work can be very lucrative. In 2001 (most recent year's statistics available), SAG members made $563 million in commercials as compared to $614.7 million made in television shows and $449.5 million from actors in motion pictures. So, more money was made by actors in commercials than in motion pictures! For their ads, many actors are paid high into six figures and beyond. Even completely unknown actors can make five to six figures for one commercial.

Something else to take into consideration: An important difference between having a "guest shot" (someone who isn't on a particular show regularly) on entertainment programming, and having a commercial airing, is that whereas the TV show will usually air a few times a year, a commercial may air many times a day. Payments for re-airings of a TV show are called "residuals"; in commercial acting they're called "use-fees." In effect, they are one and the same.

For acting in a SAG or AFTRA commercial, a principal player on-camera will make a minimum of $535 for each day's work. Payment for the first airing of a "Class-A" spot—one that airs in over twenty cities and sponsors a TV program on a network—is included as part of the fee you received up-front for the shooting. The figures below are payments for each 13-week cycle. After each cycle concludes, the payments start over again. For the same "Class-A" spot, minimum payments for use-fees are as follows.

2nd airing:	$122.70
3rd-13th airing:	$97.35 (per airing)
14th airing and thereafter:	$46.65 (per airing)

There are many classifications for commercials. Each time the commercial airs, you'll be paid, unless it's a "wild spot" (meaning it is sold separately to each market—non-network). In the case of a "wild spot" commercial, you would be paid a flat sum, in 13-week cycles, no matter how many times it airs in those 13 weeks. The use-fee amount depends on how many cities it airs in, the number of television households in those areas, among other points. The commercial can also air on cable or on the Internet.

Before you decide you want to make a commercial or two a year to give you plenty of money to live on, keep reading because the plot thickens. It is true that if you could make a few "Class-A" commercials a year that end up on the air, you could probably make a pretty decent living.

Unfortunately, just because you shoot a commercial, doesn't necessarily mean you will see it on the air. Before millions of dollars are spent putting it on the air, the commercial will be "test marketed" before audiences to see how effective it is. You would still be paid for the day's work if a commercial you shot doesn't end up on the air, but you lose out on the real money made in "use-fees."

Getting into Commercial Auditions

To get into commercial auditions, you must have an agent. Agents for commercials are obtained in the same manner as other agents. And generally it is easier to obtain a commercial agent as opposed to a theatrical one. Commercial agents represent many more actors than do their theatrical counterparts. A large number of actors have a great commercial agent and a not-so-hot theatrical agent. Many actors who have a commercial agent don't even have a theatrical one. It's not that they haven't tried.

Send your photo and resume package to commercial casting directors. Names and business addresses of these casting directors are in publications sold at Samuel French. This is kind of a long shot, but you might get a general interview with a casting director. And if she really likes you, it's possible she might even refer you to an agent. I admit it doesn't happen very often, but you're going to pursue all avenues in your quest for work, aren't you?

There are so many commercial auditions all over Los Angeles and New York that no actor is able to keep up with what is being cast and where. (If you're trying to decide where you want to act in commercials, know that over 50 percent of union commercials are cast in Los Angeles.) Even if you could keep up with it all, you still wouldn't be able to get yourself into the auditions anyway. (I'm basing my discussion here on commercials cast in New York, Chicago, and Los Angeles—the major commercial markets. There are many commercials cast in other cities. In cities that have union and union/association agents, and even ones that don't, actors should still try to get hooked up with an agent. Most advertising agencies and casting directors prefer to deal with agents.)

Many commercial casting calls do not appear on Breakdown Services. Commercial casting directors in Los Angeles and New York tend to phone a few of their favorite commercial agents directly to let them know what types they need for a commercial. This may help you understand why you'll get few, if any, commercial auditions in Los Angeles and/or New York without an agent.

The wide use of computers has led to a new trend in commercial casting in Los Angeles, where commercial agents are now submitting actors' photos to commercial casting directors online through a service known as L.A. Casting. Only an agent or manager may access this service; one more reason why you need commercial representation.

In Los Angeles, in particular, most advertising agencies hire an independent casting director for each commercial. These casting directors are running from one ad to the next and rarely have time to chat with actors. It's different in New York where many advertising agencies have casting directors on staff. This means they are more likely to set up some general interviews, though usually an agent needs to book the appointment for you.

Before searching for a commercial agent, know what type you are. There is a place for you in the commercial acting field, whether you're big, small, bald, hairy, plump, or skinny. Commercials use every conceivable type. Be what you are!

Once you've decided what type you are and have a headshot to represent that type, start sending your headshot and/or three-quarter shot out to commercial agents. You should still attach a resume to the photo. It's a big mistake to think that you don't need a resume for commercial acting. Agents and commercial casting directors want to see the resume. These days commercial acting is much more natural than it used to be, so being "real" is the trend.

Reread the chapter on resume preparation and you'll remember not to list any commercials. Even so, you can't be in any commercial that conflicts with a competing product, until you have been released from the other product's commercial. Don't even try! By listing any products on your resume, the ad agency might think you haven't been released from a competing product's ad, when in fact you might have, and not consider you. In the major markets, I can't think of any positive reason to list on a commercial resume the commercials in which you have performed. (In the smaller markets, it's more customary for agents to have their actors list commercials. You should do what is the norm in your particular area.)

If you have a commercial that isn't airing, but you're still being "held" for it, you'll still be paid. This money is called a "holding fee," which is a fee paid to the actor to "hold" him to that product— meaning he can't perform in any commercial for a competitor, until he has been released. This holding fee is compensation for that fact and because you are not making any "use-fee" money on the commercial since it isn't presently airing. For every 13 weeks you're being held, you'll be paid the holding fee which is equal to your "session" fee for that commercial (one day's pay). Ad agencies can hold you for 21 months. After that time, if the ad agency wants to keep holding you, it has to renegotiate your contract if your agent or you have timely notified the producer.

During the Audition

When she has an audition set up for you, your commercial agent will phone you. At that time, the agent will probably give you a few sentences' description of the character for which you'll be auditioning. Then, you would want to dress as the character would dress.

By the time you receive information about a character it may have been so diluted that it is totally inaccurate. The account executive at the ad agency told the producer of the commercial what the ad agency is looking for. The producer interprets that information, adds some of his own, and discusses it with the director. The director interprets the information given him, adds some of his own, and tells the casting director what he's looking for. The casting director does some interpreting in turn, adds some of her own, and informs the agent about the character. The information goes through more interpretation by the agent who, adds some of her own, and passes it to you.

So you can see that by the time the information gets to you, it could be dead wrong! You then interpret that wrong information, add some of your own, and start making decisions about the character. A situation like this came up when I was directing a national commercial where we needed women's-libber types. I requested the casting director to have the agents send actors in a suit—they needed to present a very strong businesswoman type. When I walked into the lobby of the audition room I soon discovered that something was amiss. Most of the women were wearing thong-bikini bathing suits! Agents in Los Angeles, having watched too many BAYWATCH episodes, thought "suit" meant bathing suit. Funny thing is, the male clients never complained and didn't even bring the manner of dress up until the end of the first day of auditioning.

So, before you head off for that commercial audition (or any audition for that matter), realize that you may not have the most accurate information about the type of character(s) we're looking for. It's a good idea to bring different types of clothing in the trunk of your car to every audition, whether it's for commercials or TV and film. When you arrive at the audition and read the script, you might find yourself heading back out to your car to change clothes. This will happen to you more than you think. Of course, this works great for actors in Los Angeles. New York actors, on the other hand, need to keep some extra clothes nearby—either in their apartment if it's close to the audition, or in some type of briefcase, bag, etc.

Arrive early. If for some reason you haven't been able to obtain a copy of the script from your agent or the websites previously mentioned, here's your chance to rehearse.

When you first walk into a commercial audition, you'll fill in the "sign-in" sheet, listing your name, agent, time you arrived, and Social Security number or union membership number. For SAG and AFTRA commercials, if the advertising agency or casting director keeps you over an hour, after the first hour you'll be paid $33.45 in half-hour increments, whether it was the initial audition or the first callback. (For third interviews and thereafter, you are paid starting from the first hour.)

In other words, for an audition that lasted an hour and five minutes, you'll be paid $33.45. An audition that lasted for an hour and thirty-five minutes, you'll be paid $66.90, and so on. SAG and AFTRA will have a record of how long you were on the audition because you sign out the time you leave on the "sign-in" sheet, which will be sent to them; your payment if you're kept overtime will come by check weeks later. (The above amounts are standard rates set by SAG and AFTRA and are not negotiable. The rates apply to any SAG or AFTRA commercial be it local, syndicated, cable, or network.)

This doesn't mean that if you were kept three minutes over an hour and no check shows up that you should contact SAG and demand payment. It's not worth worrying about the few dollars for a minute or two of overtime; if you do, it may not sit too well with the casting director and the director who are responsible for keeping the audition running on time. We shouldn't abuse you either. If you are more than a few minutes over, that's a different story.

A commercial being shot in a small city might be a non-union commercial. This being the case, you'll probably receive a flat fee for the commercial and no "use-fees." It's almost certain there will be no payments for overtime at an audition. (Note: If you're a member of SAG, you can't perform in a non-union commercial whether it is shot on tape or film. The same is true for AFTRA members.)

In the waiting room, there might be a "storyboard." A storyboard is a visualization of the entire commercial, with little drawings of each scene. It's the concept of the commercial, which everyone has pretty much agreed upon. If a storyboard is available, look it over carefully. Check out the expressions on the character's faces, and so on.

After signing your name and other vital statistics, you'll give your package to whomever is going to escort you from the lobby into the actual audition room. If the director is present in the audition room he might ask for your photo and resume. Then, there might be a few minutes of chitchat. We want to learn something about your personality; we want to determine whether you are likable before we cast you in a commercial. We know that if the public doesn't like the actors in a commercial, that commercial won't be very successful.

On commercial auditions the actor should be "up," meaning he or she should have lots of energy. A sense of humor is always a plus. I'm sorry to have to admit this, but we're pretty bored in commercial auditions. We've seen hundreds of actors day after day, all reading the same few lines over and over, and when someone can come in and help us to laugh, we appreciate it.

Being laid-back on a commercial audition is a killer. If it appears as though you just went to a Quaalude festival, you can forget being cast. Be bright and happy. Be friendly and act as though you are having a terrific time, even though you would just as soon be at a funeral. Don't let us know that you hate the product you are trying to sell, even if you do. You might be tempted to look at the hamburger in a fast-food commercial and wonder whether to eat it, or set it free. If we do bring food in as a prop (which is rare), it has probably been sitting around all day and might appear to be nuclear waste. You must act as though the product is truly wonderful, although it might remind you of a science project. (If it makes you feel any better, we're most likely feeling the same thing!)

Assuming the audition is recorded, and almost all commercial auditions are, you'll be asked to "hit your mark." This means positioning your body right over an "X" or a "T" usually marked on the floor with tape. If it's a "T," then one foot should parallel one side of the vertical line of the "T" and the other foot the other side of it, with both feet behind the horizontal line. If it's an "X" then center your body over the center of the "X." Don't be like many actors and be sloppy about it. We directors look to see how you "hit" that mark, because if you can't hit a mark correctly we're going to have some serious problems on the set. It means the lighting will be off, the framing askew, and the focus "soft." Hitting the mark is one indication of how much you know about screen acting.

The shooting will have you on camera for only a few minutes at most. You'll be asked to "slate." This simply means, when the camera rolls, you state your name and, usually, that of your agent. You might or might not be asked to show your profiles.

The slate is the most important part of your audition. Let's be honest here: When we're recording hundreds of actors daily for a national commercial, I hope you don't think we actually sit down each evening and watch every actor's complete commercial. What happens is that we fast-forward from slate to slate to slate to slate, and so on. (This is sometimes true for TV and film auditions, also.) On a really good day we might watch anywhere from five to ten actual full commercials.

"Unfair," you respond? Go back to my earlier stated fact: This is an unfair business, always has been, always will be. So forget "fair."

We are looking for two things in that slate: First, warmth. Everyone looks so serious. Lighten up! We're not doing *Hamlet* . . . . we're selling Ding-Dongs and Ho-Ho's! SMILE. Secondly, did we understand your name? This may sound basic, but for every ten people we want to call back, there are at least two we can't because we don't know who they are. Actors have lost a callback or even a job because when they spoke their name they were less understandable than the Dalai Lama.

Actors shouldn't throw their names out quickly, thinking this part isn't very important. They are wrong! As mentioned, when it comes to viewing playbacks, it's the most important part of the entire audition. How many times have you come home, turned on your answering machine and heard something like this, "My name is TGTTVL and my phone number is 7★&#5#%"? Same thing happens in auditions, and it drives us nuts.

After the slate, pause for three or four seconds before you begin the reading. When we are viewing the playbacks, immediately following an actor's slate, there's a little discussion about them. I'll hear such things as, "Her hair is beautiful," or "Wow, check out the nose," etc. I used to time this quick discussion after each actor, with a stopwatch. The average discussion lasts 3.2 seconds; hence, the pause.

(Yes, I did say that this book is a business book and not a "How to act" book. But the director in me makes me mention the above and its importance.)

You might be asked to deliver a scripted commercial or to do an "improv"; meaning that you act out the commercial on the spot using your own thoughts and dialogue. If you do an improv, be different. Don't be boring. Humor is always welcomed. (If you are to be requested to improvise dialogue, legally by SAG and AFTRA contract regulations you should be notified in advance and paid a small fee. Your agent will have the details.)

During the audition you may be asked if you have a certain skill. We might, for instance, need a skydiver for a particular commercial. If you can't skydive, then don't say you can! Everyone involved with the commercial will eventually find out anyway.

When I was an actor way back when the Big Mac was introduced, I was auditioning for a Honda commercial and was asked if I could drive a motorcycle. I was, and still am, scared to death of those death traps, but in my eagerness for the job, I said I could.

I was cast in the commercial. When we started shooting, I ran over the director's foot. He limped around without much of a sense of humor all day, and after the shooting swung by St. Joseph's Hospital for X-rays. I had broken his foot. I never got to work for that director again.

You'll sign out giving the time on the "sign-in" sheet as you leave the audition. Generally, you'll hear from your agent within a few days or so if you are wanted for a callback. Sometimes the recorded auditions will have to be sent to the director and/or the ad agency, one or both of which may be located in another city. In this case, it may be a week or so before they view them, so there will be a delay before you are informed about a callback.

Commercial Callbacks

As is the case with any callback, whether for TV, film, or commercials, don't drastically change your appearance. Dress and act the same way you did on the original audition or you thwart the reason you were called back. Sometimes actors want to come on the callback dressed differently and sporting a different kind of character in their reading, because they think by doing this that they show variety;

everyone will see how versatile they are. Wrong! The exception to this, of course, would be if you were called back for a totally different role. But even then the way you presented yourself in the original audition, may be why we thought you were right for the new role for which you are auditioning.

Wearing the same clothes makes them a part of the identity of the actor. For instance, I might say to the casting director, "Where is that women that was in the blue shirt with the tan collar?" I don't mean your clothes should stand out in any way, but sometimes we do identify someone by what they were wearing.

We're not necessarily looking for versatile actors. We're looking for the perfect actor for this part only. If you're called back, you must closely resemble what we're looking for. Each time you come in you might meet different people. These people might have been told by the people you originally saw how right you are for the part, based on your original performance. If you come in now totally different for the new people, the new people might wonder what kind of medication the people who originally saw you were on.

There's really no way to specifically prepare for a particular callback, unless you "accidentally" walked off with the script they gave you at the original audition! The callback is usually similar to the original audition, but fewer people are now in competition for the part. For a union commercial audition callback that goes over an hour, you'll still be paid $33.45 in half-hour increments.

If you are called a third time (second callback), you'll be paid $133.75 for showing up and if the agency keeps you for over two hours, you'll be paid $33.45 for each half-hour over the two. And if you're called a fourth time (third callback), you'll be paid $267.50 for any time up to four hours. (All of the above amounts are standard rates and aren't negotiable.) It's rare for ad agencies to have two callbacks or to keep you for over an hour. Normally, commercials are cast from the first callback (second audition), and sometimes even from the playbacks of the original audition.

Unions and Commercials

If you are cast in a SAG commercial as a "principal player," you are eligible to join SAG, provided the company shooting the commercial is a signatory of SAG. In commercial work, if the actor is on-camera and is identified with the product, demonstrates the product, reacts to the message in the commercial, or performs a stunt, he might be considered a principal player without ever mouthing a word. If the ad agency considers an actor an extra, but the actor himself thinks by the above definition he is a principal player, he can file a claim with SAG; the commercial contracts department will view the commercial in question and make a determination.

To recap, if you've earned less than $3,500 in the first 151 days, or have earned no money in commercials in 120 days, or if after the first five months you haven't earned at least $3,500 in any 91-day period, you can release yourself from your union commercial agency contract. (ATA and NATR agents do not necessarily follow these guidelines.)

Voice-Overs

This isn't a book about voice-overs so we'll touch on the basics here. If you plan to work seriously in voice-overs, you should read some of the many fine books out there that cover them exclusively, and take some serious voice-over workshops. This is an extremely hard field to break into and not, as many newcomers think, a sideline. And it is still dominated by male actors. It is becoming a tougher field to enter because many stars are now doing voice-over work. Frankly, many of them need the money. As for animated films, stars sell more tickets.

One advantage of voice-over work is that you can sometimes have product conflicts that are legal. You usually aren't as associated with the product in a voice-over as you are when you're in front of the camera. The general rule of thumb is that the voices between the two competing products must not be identifiable with each other. So, if you did a character voice in one ad, and a straight voice in a competing ad, this might be perfectly legal. However, you must clear this product conflict with the companies for which you are working.

There's an abundance of work for voice-over actors—commercials, cartoons, TV narration, radio, dubbing foreign films into English, dubbing English films into foreign languages, recording of novels, narration for educational and industrial films, computer games, to name some possibilities. Voice-over work calls for a very specialized talent, where you have to be able to use your voice well to get cast in this field. It's not a field that the beginner can jump right into, but one where proven professionals are used.

Obtaining a Voice-Over Agent

Use many of the principles for getting work as a visible actor in obtaining work as a voice-over actor (radio and otherwise). For instance, you must obtain an agent, although there are differences between obtaining an agent for the visual acting fields and one for voice-over areas.

Most voice-over agents are associated with commercial agents. Some large commercial agencies have a separate department specifically for voice-over work. Check with commercial agents and ask if they have a voice-over department, or even better, obtain a copy of *The Agencies*, from the drama bookstores previously mentioned. It will inform you specifically which agencies have voice-over departments.

To seek representation, send agents your resume and a CD of your voice. In this situation, don't send a photo, because it might give them a preconceived and wrong impression of your voice than it actually sounds. Do not make a CD that sounds homemade! If you do the recording yourself, make sure it sounds professional. It's really better that you don't make the CD yourself! An amateur-sounding recording is to the voice-over industry what a bad photograph is to the theatrical/commercial industry; it does more harm than good. There are plenty of sound studios around the country that specialize in this type of recording.

Do readings of material that best suit your voice—commercial readings, animated voices, etc. The CD shouldn't be over five minutes in length. Each "scene" should be short. We get the idea about your voice in each new sequence in a very short period of time. Directors will have time to listen to a very small portion only, so put your best work first. If the listeners don't like what they hear at the very beginning, the CD will be turned off very quickly.

Once you have an agent, he'll be submitting this CD to casting directors for potential jobs. On rare occasions, an actor might be cast right from his CD.

For many actors, commercials are the end. Some actors only want to be in commercials, and some are extremely successful at it. For other actors, commercials are a way to make money while waiting for that "big break."

CHAPTER SIXTEEN
That's a Wrap

Two guys are sitting in a bar and one says to the other, "I've got an IQ of 160." The other says, "You gotta be kidding. I've got 159." So they start talking about Einstein's Relativity Theory.

The two guys sitting next to them overhear the conversation, and one says to the other, "I've got an IQ of 150." The other says, "You gotta be kidding. I've got 149." So they start talking about Porsches, Mercedes Benzes....

Two more guys overhear the conversation and one says to the other, "I've got an IQ of 60." The other very slowly says, "You gotta be kidding. I've got 55....Been on any auditions lately?"

Don't believe this joke for a minute. That's just what it is—a joke. By now, I think you can understand that being able to act isn't good enough. An actor's brain cells can't be on the Endangered Species List because you have to understand the business to be successful in this industry. Wanting to be a working actor but not understanding the business of show business would be akin to being a cordless bungee-jumper.

The mere fact that you took the time to read this book is evidence that you at least have some determination. From what you've read you should know what to look out for in this business. I hope I have been of some help to you; you have been to me—you bought my book. But I know that what you've learned will save you a lot of time, trouble, and money.

I suggested in the Introduction that after reading this book about the industry, you should read all the other books out there on this subject; that all of them have something to offer. The acting business is not a science and there are as many opinions out there as there are people. The insights I hope I've given you are from the director's point of view, the director's view being important because in most cases he's the one most likely to be casting you.

For a healthy attitude you need the characteristics of determination, hard work, a strong will, loads of confidence, respect for others, some luck, and a complete understanding of the Beverly Theory. But even actors can't live on an inspired attitude alone. For laying a foundation, there are a few essentials, which may seem obvious but deserve a brief mention.

Logistics

Wherever you are planning to work, you'll first need lodging. A street address is preferable, but if you're living in Central Park, at least obtain a post office box. If you're moving to Los Angeles or New York from a smaller city, you will be in for a real shock when looking for a place to live. If you're broke more often than a New Year's resolution—normal status for actors—looking for an apartment in either of those cities will probably rank on your "fun list" right up there with a prostrate exam. The first thing you learn when you arrive in Los Angeles or New York is that the term "fair housing" has nothing to do with the price. You'll pay a fortune for an apartment so small that the mice are hunchbacked, and your dog will have to wag its tail up and down.

Not only that, the apartments are usually so poorly constructed that it appears they were built in wood shop. Especially because of actors' hours, be very careful that you reside in a safe area. Some neighborhoods are so tough that Godzilla is considered effeminate.

Since you are going to have to pay for that lodging and other necessities, you'll need income. If you're not endowed with a comfortable inheritance, this means a job. It helps to be the recipient of parental asset infusion (money from mom or dad). Over 90 percent of the Screen Actors Guild membership rely on outside income to make a living. Unfortunately, auditions are usually held in the daytime hours. So you either must have a job that permits you to leave upon request during the day, or take a night job. Ask just about anyone in Hollywood what he does for a living; when he says, "I'm an actor," ask him, "What restaurant?" Yes, many actors become waiters while looking for that big break. But you'll find that actors come from all walks of life.

Number three, you'll need a telephone and something that can take messages—an answering machine, an answering service, or a cell phone with messaging capability. Many are the times I've tried to get a hold of an actor and his telephone just rings and rings. People in this industry don't have the time to keep phoning until you happen to be there to answer.

Basically, you need to have the appearance of a secure person. You want nothing to present you as a total failure as a human being. So find a place to live, have an income, and secure a telephone and answering service of some type.

Despite my comments, I'm not meaning to play down the talent end of the acting business. Talent is very important, but talent alone will do you little good, if any, without a winning personality and a good business knowledge of how the entertainment industry works.

A Good Attitude

A good attitude is as important in this field as it is in others. Attitude is involved in the way you treat the people around you. I haven't yet figured out why so many actors in press interviews admit to how awful they are to their fellow human beings. Some even talk about how they order everyone around on the set. Let's face it: When people in Hollywood pat you on the back, they're figuring where to stick the knife.

You'll meet people in this business who are as stuck-up as a billboard and could have their egos apply for statehood. A great number of stars in Los Angeles are going into debt trying to keep up with people who already are in debt. Their heads get too big for their toupees. Maybe you are standing in their aura. Don't stand in their aura. Don't get taken in by the stars, directors, and producers who are suffering from rectal-cranial inversion.

These people have a lot of karma to burn off. They should buy fire instead of life insurance; there's no doubt where they're going—they can skip the harp lessons. I see no advantage in treating people badly, and it's no strange coincidence that many of these same actors have a hard time finding work when, perhaps, their TV show is canceled—which it ultimately will be! Then they're really in trouble because it takes more money to live beyond your means than it used to.

Some of these people are on top of the world, but someone needs to remind them that it turns every twenty-four hours. Movie stars and diapers should be changed regularly—and for the same reason. If you think you're indispensable, stick your finger in a bowl of water. Now remove it. See the impression you made?

As I mentioned earlier, directors have a kind of nice term for actors that are hard to work with—"Difficult." No director I know likes to work with difficult actors. The fact that no one understands their behavior doesn't make them an artist! We need to bear in mind that old Hollywood saying: *Be nice to the people on your way up because you're going to see them again on your way down.*

"Character" Does Count

Don't be fooled by all the publicity. I know that this industry gets a bad rap as far as "character" is concerned. When an actor is caught with drugs, it is in every newspaper in the entire world. When a star has a messy divorce, it is reported on every newsmagazine show and makes print headlines. In this business, unfortunately, there's no such thing as bad publicity—unless it's your obituary. Yes, it's true show business has its fair share of these problems. In fact, if you go to a Hollywood PTA meeting, there'll be 300 parents for 10 kids.

Every profession has people with drug problems and messy divorces. The acting profession is not at the top of the lists when it comes to those problems, you might be surprised to learn.

Most directors don't tolerate any drug or serious alcohol usage from actors. If we suspect such a thing, we may insert a clause into the actor's contract that will allow us to drug test him at any time during the shoot. I have never, and will never, entertain the use of any recreational drugs and I expect my cast and crew to adhere to that policy while under my stewardship. Anyone who has not or does not, I have fired, and will continue to fire.

An actor coming into an audition hung over from drugs or alcohol can forget winning that role. I'll not only refuse to call him back, but I'll personally phone his agent and ask that agent to drop the actor as a client. That said, I can honestly add I've seen so little of this on my sets that it's barely worth mentioning. It just makes me feel better to include my moral statement here.

That the public perceives everyone in Hollywood to be wild and crazy, comes from the media. Actors do sometimes see successful actors on drugs and alcohol, so they think it's okay. And, yes, some actors have had enough alcohol to rub down the Dallas Cowboys. Those actors usually didn't start out that way or they wouldn't have been cast in much, if anything.

Another impression as old as the hills is the "casting couch" idea. But frankly, this "sexual favor" thing isn't something I see much in this business, at least among legit people. My career is on the line with every show that I direct. Very few, if any, legitimate directors would risk their careers for a few sexual favors. If you come across the casting couch routine, it probably won't be from directors or casting directors. I'm not saying it can't happen, but more likely it will be from underlings who don't have as much to risk as the director, producer, and casting director.

And while we're on sex, don't do porn! The idea that you can begin working as a porn star and then move into legitimate TV and film work is ridiculous. It doesn't happen. Stay away from this type of production if you want to have a legitimate film or TV acting career.

Final Words

Whatever you do—relax. Therapy is expensive; popping bubble wrap is cheap. You choose. Getting all depressed and bent out of shape will only defeat your purposes, and we feel that attitude coming from you in auditions. If a certain agent doesn't take you on as a client, you'll find another agent. If one of us big, bad, ugly directors doesn't want you for a certain part, you'll find another part. Granted, it is sometimes hard to keep a positive attitude under circumstances where you're rejected so much, but you must learn to cope with it.

In my acting days, I was sometimes out of work. To keep me from going insane, I would call in sick to places I didn't even work. I once called the Sears headquarters and said, "This is Tom Logan and I am not coming in today." A secretary asked me why not. I argued with her and I didn't even work there:

"What department do you work in?" she inquired.

"Ah . . . . shipping," I cleverly responded.

She answered sternly, "I'm going to put the shipping clerk on right away."

I said, "You just go right ahead!"

Two minutes later I heard a voice saying to me, "Tom, I understand you're not coming in today."

"I don't feel well," was my response.

"Do you have a doctor's note?" he asked.

"No." I answered.

"We're going to dock your pay," he threatened.

I responded with, "But I have a wife, two kids . . . . "

When you get down on your career, find something to do that

perks you up. Calling in sick to places where I didn't even work did it for me. And being an actor, turning down "work" even made it more fun. Think of something that you enjoy doing and that will perk you up when you start practicing the "actor's routine." Life is short. Enjoy life. Think of all the women who passed up the dessert on the Hindenburg!

You have to accept the reality of show business, but that shouldn't stop you from being optimistic. Know you have something to offer the public. Facing reality with a positive attitude is better than living in a fantasy that someone will "discover" you. "Discover" yourself. I hear people say it takes luck to make it in this business. I believe in luck—how else can we explain the successes of the people we dislike? But you also make your own luck by hard work. Perhaps there is a certain part of luck you have no control over. So when, or if, you get that lucky break, be prepared for it by studying your craft.

Let me tell you a little secret about every star in this business. Stars are always wondering whether they are really stars because they're talented, or because they're lucky. I submit that it's a combination of the two.

This may sound offbeat, but follow my recommendation and watch episodes of *E True Hollywood Story* on the E network. After watching a few episodes, you'll come away realizing how hard these people have worked to get where they are in this business. Besides being entertaining, this show will enlighten you about how acting careers began and have, or have not, sustained.

You may never become a household name, but if you follow the principles I've set forth in this book, chances are that you'll eventually get work as a professional actor. The odds are in your favor. It's a numbers game. In auditions, if we see an average—there is no real "average"—of three hundred people for a part, then you should have a job in three hundred auditions. So the longer you hang in there, the better the numbers become for you.

Above all forget that you want to be a "star." If becoming a star is meant to happen to you, then in due time it will. Otherwise, feel proud that you will accomplish what many people only dream of—to work in the greatest profession in the world—acting.

You will eventually find work as an actor. Even if you do everything wrong in auditions, you will still eventually get cast. *Even a broken clock is right twice a day!*

See ya on the set!

Appendices

List of Websites

www.acapd.org	Academy Players Directory
www.actorsequity.org	Actors' Equity Association
www.aftra.org	American Federation of Television and Radio Artists
www.agentassociation.com	Association of Talent Agents
www.backstage.com	Backstage Magazine
www.breakdownservices.com	Breakdown Services
www.castnet.com	Castnet
www.dga.org	Directors Guild of America
www.hollywoodreporter.com	Hollywood Reporter
www.imdb.com	Internet Movie Database
www.sag.org	Screen Actors Guild
www.showfax.com	Showfax
www.variety.com	Variety

APPENDIX B
List of SAG Offices

LOS ANGELES:
5757 Wilshire Boulevard
Los Angeles, CA 90036
323-954-1600

NEW YORK:
360 Madison Avenue, 12th Floor
New York, NY 10017
212-944-1030

ARIZONA: *(Can Assist Utah)*
1616 East Indian School Road,
    Suite 330
Phoenix, AZ 85016
602-265-2712

BOSTON:
535 Boylston Street
Boston, MA 02116
617-262-8001

CHICAGO: *(North Region Office)*
1 East Erie Street, Suite 650
Chicago, IL 60611
312-573-8081

CLEVELAND:
1468 West 9th Street, #720
Cleveland, OH 44113
216-579-9305

COLORADO: *(The Colorado
    District Office works in conjunction
    with the North Region Office in
    Chicago.)*
Market Square Center
1400 Sixteenth Street, Suite 400
Denver, CO 80202
720-932-8193

DALLAS:
6060 N. Central Expressway
Suite 302, LB 604
Dallas, TX 75206
214-363-8300

DETROIT: *(The Detroit District
    Office works in conjunction with
    the North Region Office in
    Chicago)*
American Center
27777 Franklin Road, Suite 300
Southfield, MI 48034
248-213-0272

FLORIDA: *(Central)*
Southhall Center
101 Southhall Lane, Suite 405
Maitland, FL 32751
407-667-4835

FLORIDA: *(Miami)*
7300 North Kendall Drive,
    Suite 620
Miami, FL 33156
305-670-7677
    (Miami is also the South Region
    Office, covering Alabama, Arkansas,
    Georgia, Louisiana, Maryland,
    Mississippi, North Carolina, Ok-
    lahoma, Puerto Rico, South Car-
    olina, Tennessee, Texas, Virginia,
    West Virginia, and Washington,
    D.C.)

GEORGIA:
455 East Paces Ferry Road NE,
    Suite 334
Atlanta, GA 30305
404-239-0131

HAWAII:
949 Kapiolani Boulevard, #105
Honolulu, HI 96814
808-596-0388

HOUSTON:
2020 North Loop, W., Suite 240
Houston, TX 77018
713-686-4614

MINNEAPOLIS/ST. PAUL:
708 North First Street, Suite 333
Minneapolis, MN 55401
612-371-9120

NASHVILLE:
P.O. Box 121087
Nashville, TN 37212
615-327-2944

NEVADA:
3960 Howard Hughes Parkway,
    Suite 500
Las Vegas, NV 89109
702-737-8818

NORTH CAROLINA:
    (Office is in Altanta)
Tower Place Center
3340 Peachtree Road NE,
    Suite 1800
Atlanta, GA 30326
404-812-5342

PHILADELPHIA:
230 South Broad Street,
    10th Floor
Philadelphia, PA 19102
215-545-3150

PORTLAND:
3030 Southwest Moody,
    Suite 104
Portland, OR 97201
503-279-9600

SAN DIEGO:
7867 Convoy Court, Suite 307
San Diego, CA 92111
858-278-7695

SAN FRANCISCO:
350 Sansome Street, Suite 900
San Francisco, CA 94104
415-391-7510

SEATTLE:
Screen Actors Guild/Seattle
4000 Aurora Ave., N. #102
Seattle, WA 98103
206-270-0493

ST. LOUIS:
1310 Papin Street, Suite 103
St. Louis, MO 63103
314-231-8410

WASHINGTON, D.C.
4340 East West Highway,
   Suite 204
Bethesda, MD 20814
301-657-2560

List of AFTRA Offices

NATIONAL OFFICE—NEW YORK:
260 Madison Avenue, 7th Floor
New York, NY 10016
212-532-0800

NATIONAL OFFICE—LOS ANGELES:
5757 Wilshire Boulevard, 9th Floor
Los Angeles, CA 90036
323-634-8100

Aftra Locals And Chapters:

ATLANTA:
455 East Paces Ferry Road, NE,
　　Suite 334
Atlanta, GA 30305
404-239-0131

BUFFALO:
WIVB-TV
2077 Elmwood Avenue
Buffalo, NY 14207
716-879-4989

BOSTON:
535 Boylston Street
Boston, MA 02116
617-262-8001

CHICAGO:
One East Erie Street, Suite 650
Chicago, IL 60611
312-573-8081

CLEVELAND:
1468 West 9th Street, Suite 720
Cleveland, OH 44113
216-781-2255

DALLAS/FT. WORTH:
6060 N. Central Expressway
Suite 302. L.B. 604
Dallas, TX 75206
214-363-8300

DENVER:
1400 16th Street, Suite 400
Denver, CO 80222
720-932-8193

DETROIT:
27777 Franklin Road, Suite 300
Southfield, MI 48034
248-213-0264

FRESNO:
C/O AFTRA National
260 Madison Avenue,
    7th Floor
New York, NY 10016
212-532-0800

HAWAII:
C/O AFTRA National
260 Madison Avenue, 7th Floor
New York, NY 10016
866-634-8100 (toll free)

HOUSTON:
2020 North Loop W., Suite 240
Houston, TX 77018
713-686-4614

KANSAS CITY:
P.O. Box 32167
4000 Baltimore, 2nd Floor
Kansas City, MO 64111
816-753-4557

LOS ANGELES:
SEE ABOVE

MIAMI:
2750 North 29th Avenue,
    Suite 200N
Hollywood, FL 33020
954-920-2476

NASHVILLE:
P.O. Box 121087
1108 17th Avenue South
Nashville, TN 37212
615-327-2944

NEW ORLEANS:
(Office in Texas)
2400 Augusta Drive, Suite 264
Houston, TX 77057
866-236-2941 (toll free from
    Louisiana only)
713-972-1806

NEW YORK:
SEE ABOVE

OMAHA:
3000 Franham Street,
    Suite 3 East
Omaha, NE 68131
402-346-8384

PEORIA:
C/O AFTRA National Office
260 Madison Avenue,
    7th Floor
New York, NY 10016
800-638-6796

PHILADELPHIA:
230 South Broad Street,
    Suite 500
Philadelphia, PA 19102
215-732-0507

PHOENIX:
1616 East Indian School Road,
    Suite 330
Phoenix, AZ 85016
602-265-2712

PITTSBURGH:
625 Stanwix Street
Pittsburgh, PA 15222
412-281-6767

PORTLAND:
3030 Southwest Moody,
    Suite #104
Portland, OR 97201
503-279-9600

ROCHESTER:
C/O AFTRA National
260 Madison Avenue, 7th Floor
New York, NY 10016
585-467-7982

SACRAMENTO/
    STOCKTON:
8145 La Riviera Drive
Sacramento, CA 95826
916-387-5129

SAN DIEGO:
7867 Convoy Court, Suite 307
San Diego, CA 92111
858-278-7695

SAN FRANCISCO:
350 Sansome Street, Suite 900
San Francisco, CA 94104
415-391-7510

SCHENECTADY/ALBANY:
1400 Balltown Road
Schenectady, NY 12309
518-346-6666

WGY-AM/WRVE-FM
1 Washington Square
Albany, NY 11205
518-452-4800

SEATTLE:
4000 Aurora Avenue, Suite 102
Seattle, WA 98103
206-282-2506

ST. LOUIS:
1310 Papin Street, Suite 103
St. Louis, MO 63103
314-231-8410

TRI-STATE: *(Includes Cincinnati, Columbus & Dayton, OH; Indianapolis, IN and Louisville, KY)*
920-A Race Street, 2nd Floor
Cincinnati, OH 45202
513-579-8668

TWIN CITIES:
708 North First Street
Suite 333—Itasca Building
Minneapolis, MN 55401
612-371-9120

WASHINGTON D.C./ BALTIMORE:
4340 East West Highway, Suite 204
Bethesda, MD 20814
301-657-2560

List of Equity Offices

NEW YORK:
165 West 46th Street
New York, NY 10036
212-869-8530

LOS ANGELES:
5757 Wilshire Boulevard, Suite 1
Los Angeles, CA 90035
323-634-1750

CHICAGO:
125 South Clark Street, Suite 1500
Chicago, IL 60603
312-641-0393

ORLANDO, FLORIDA:
10319 Orangewood Boulevard
Orlando, FL 32821
407-345-8600

SAN FRANCISCO:
350 Sansome Street, Suite 900
San Francisco, CA 94104
415-391-3838

Eligibility Requirements for Joining SAG

How Do I Qualify to Join SAG?

A performer may become eligible for Screen Actors Guild membership under one of the following two conditions: proof of SAG employment or employment under an affiliated performers' union.

1. Proof of SAG Employment
   A. Principal Performer Employment
      Performers may join SAG upon proof of employment. Employment must be in a principal or speaking role in a SAG film, videotape, or television program or commercial. Proof of such employment may be in the form of a signed contract, a payroll check or check stub, or a letter from the company (on company letterhead). The document proving employment must provide the following information:
      - applicant's name
      - applicant's Social Security number
      - name of the production or name of the commercial (product name)
      - the salary paid (in dollar amount)
      - the specific date(s) worked
   B. Background Players Employment
      Performers may join SAG upon proof of employment as a SAG covered background player at full SAG rates and condi-

tions for a *minimum* of three workdays subsequent to March 25, 1990. Employment must be by a company signed to a SAG Background Players' Agreement, and in a SAG film, videotape, television program or commercial. Proof of such employment must be in the form of a signed employment voucher (or time card), plus an original payroll check or check stub. Such documents must provide the same information (name, Social Security number, etc.) as listed in A above.

2. Employment Under an Affiliated Performers' Union
   Performers may join SAG if the applicant is a paid-up member of an affiliated performers' union (ACTRA, AEA, AFTRA, AGMA, or AGVA) for a period of one year and has worked at least once as a principal performer in that union's jurisdiction.

What Is the Fee to Join?

To become a SAG member, the current initiation fee is $1,310, plus the first semiannual basic dues payment of $50. That makes the total fee to join $1,360.

However, fees may be lower in certain branch offices. Check with the branch you plan on joining. Joining fees are payable in full at the time of application by cashier's check or money order. However, some branches—for example, Los Angeles—do accept credit cards for payment of joining fees. Check the payment policy with the branch you plan on joining.

Under no circumstances are personal checks accepted for joining fees.

What About Annual Dues?

Dues are based on a sliding scale with the amount determined by how much you earn under SAG contracts. You are billed for one-half of the annual dues in May and the other half in November. As of 11/01/99, basic annual dues are $100. In addition, members pay 1.85 percent of earnings between $1 and $200,000, plus .5% for earnings between $200,001 and $500,000.

Falsification of Application

Your application and proof of employment will be fully investigated by the Guild. Your application for membership will be denied if you have falsified your credentials, or if your stated qualifying employment is false.

While it is your responsibility to ascertain the validity of your qualifying employment, SAG will be the sole arbiter in determining whether the employer was legitimate or not and whether the qualifying employment which you performed was actual production work or work created solely to enable you to gain Guild membership.

Please be aware that false representation or deception on your part will jeopardize your chances to join SAG. Further, if the Guild discovers such false representation or deception on your part *after* your application has been granted, you may be subject to disciplinary proceedings, which could result in your being fined, suspended and/or expelled from the Guild.

Appointments for Admission

If you meet the eligibility requirements and wish to join, contact the SAG office nearest you. *Call before you come* in so they can advise you of the amount of your joining fee and arrange an appointment with the New Membership Department.

At the time you join, you will be required to supply a photograph and you will need to sign a "photograph release form" if you wish the photo displayed on SAG's online talent search database, CastSAG.

New-Member Orientations

Most branches hold periodic new-member orientations (check with the branch you're planning to join). You should plan to attend an orientation as soon as possible after you join to learn some basic information you need to know about the Guild and the signatory producers who'll be employing you. Attending an orientation session will help you maximize your Guild membership and opportunities. Working performers will be on hand to answer any questions you may have about the industry and you'll meet other new members just starting their SAG careers.

Professional Name

SAG makes every effort to avoid having members with the same or very similar names. Therefore, the possibility the Guild may not be able to enroll you with the professional name you wish to have. They suggest that prior to your appointment to join, you choose two or three alternate names. This will facilitate the processing of your membership.

AEA Membership Information and Procedures

Eligibility To Join:

You may apply for membership by any one of the following methods:

EQUITY CONTRACT

You may join the Association by virtue of employment under an Equity contract. Applications for joining Equity are only valid during the term of the contract. Certain contract types also have a length-of-employment requirement before a membership application becomes valid; the Membership Department will advise you at the time of joining. The Equity Council may also authorize additional qualifications for membership under special circumstances.

4A'S (ASSOCIATED ACTORS AND ARTISTS OF AMERICA) AFFILIATION

Membership is also available by virtue of prior membership in a performing arts sister union (such as Screen Actors Guild or the American Federation of Television and Radio Artists). Applicants must be members in good standing of the sister union for at least one year, and must have worked as a performer under the union's jurisdiction. You must submit proof of such employment (e.g., copy of the contract or a written statement by the parent union indicating the type and date of your contract). (The sister union policy is not applicable to non-resident alien performers. See Aliens/Foreign Actor Rules below.)

EQUITY MEMBERSHIP CANDIDATE PROGRAM (EMC)

This program permits actors and stage managers-in-training to credit theatrical work in an Equity theatre towards eventual membership in Equity. After securing a position at a participating theatre, you may register as a candidate. The registration fee will be credited against any future Initiation Fee when you become eligible for membership. Eligibility under this program requires a total of 50 weeks of EMC work at participating theatres.

Application Instructions

APPLICATION FORM

Once you meet the joining requirements, complete both sides of the membership application. If you are under 18 years of age, a parent or legal guardian must also sign the application.

NAME

All performing arts unions generally prohibit the issuing of a professional name that is identical (or similar sounding) to that of an already current member of the union. If a conflict exists, you will be advised at the time that you submit an application to join Equity that you may have to change your professional name.

ALIENS/FOREIGN ACTOR RULES

There are certain eligibility restrictions that are applicable to non-resident Aliens. You will need to submit proof of US citizenship or Resident Alien status with your application for membership if you were born outside of the U.S. If you are not a U.S. citizen or U.S. Resident Alien, you may join Equity by virtue of employment under an Equity contract that was granted pursuant to valid work authorization papers. There are, however, special reciprocal membership rules between American Actors' Equity Association and Canadian Equity.

PAYMENTS

Any initiation fee payments accompanying your application should be made in the form of a certified check or money order. If you pay by personal check, your application will be held until the check clears your bank.

INITATION FEE

Equity's initiation fee is currently $1,000 and must be paid within a maximum two-year period. You are cautioned that your membership, and any monies paid, will be forfeited should you fail to complete payment of the full initiation fee within the two-year period. All membership privileges, including the right to vote and attend meetings and Equity-only auditions, commence upon the initial payment of $300 within six months of the filing of your application.

If you are working under an Equity contract at the time of joining, authorization for dues and Initiation Fee deductions from your weekly salary appears on the face of the Equity contract. Weekly deductions towards the balance due will be made from your salary according to a schedule. Please contact Equity for that schedule. The deductions will continue while you are employed until the full initiation is paid.

If you are joining Equity through 4A's affiliation or the Membership Candidate Program, the minimum $400 initial payment is due with your application.

If your parent union (the first performing artists' union you joined) is the American Guild of Musical Artists (AGMA) or Canadian Equity, you may be eligible for a reduction in the Equity Initiation Fee based on the amount of the initiation fee that you paid to your parent union. You will be advised of the amount of this re-duction by the Equity Membership Department at the time you submit your application.

DUES

Equity's dues structure has two components: Basic Dues (currently $119 as of November 2003), payable semi-annually each May and November; and Work Dues, which are deducted from weekly gross earnings. Gross earnings do not include the minimum portion of out-of-town per diem expense monies. The maximum Equity earnings subject to Work Dues (currently 2 percent of gross earnings) is $300,000 a year.

OTHER INFORMATION

Upon Equity's receipt of your contract or your application form, a package of important information, including *About Equity* and the Equity Constitution and By-Laws will be sent to you.

LOSS OF MEMBERSHIP

If you are delinquent in the payment of dues for a period of two years, and you did not apply for inactive status, you are considered out-of-benefit and membership is automatically terminated. In order to rejoin Equity, you must secure a new contract and pay a new Initiation Fee. Members are therefore strongly urged to remain in good standing with Equity.

APPENDIX G:
Equity Membership Candidate (EMC) Program

REGISTRATION

To register for the program, you must first secure a qualifying position at an Equity theatre that offers the Membership Candidate (EMC) program. Next, complete the application form supplied by the theatre and return it to them with the non-refundable $100 registration fee, payable to Actors' Equity Association.

MODIFIED EMC PROGRAM FOR 4A'S SISTER UNION MEMBERS: SAG, AFTRA, AGVA, HAU

Members of any performing arts sister union would normally be required to sign an Equity contract when working in Equity's jurisdiction. However, you may request a waiver of your professional status in order to train for the theatre by checking the appropriate box on the application form. Your application must include a copy of your resume and the $100 registration fee. This modified program allows you to work under the EMC program, you may choose to join Equity after 25 weeks, or you may continue to work the full 50 weeks as an EMC.

QUALIFYING FOR EQUITY MEMBERSHIP—50 WEEKS

- As a candidate, you must complete 50 creditable weeks of work for eligibility to join Equity.

- The 50 weeks do not have to be consecutive, and may be accumulated over any length of time at any number of Equity theatres authorized to offer the EMC Program. Be aware that there are limitations as to the types of work that can be credited under provisions of various Equity contracts. Please call the nearest Equity office if you have questions about how weeks are credited at a particular theatre.

- Once you are registered, Equity records all of your workweeks as reported by the theatre. Nonetheless, you should keep track of them yourself and notify Equity when you have 50 weeks.

COMPLETING THE PROGRAM

Upon completion of the program, your eligibility to join Equity lasts for five years. During that time, if you are engaged to work at an Equity theatre, you must be signed to an Equity contract. If you do *not* choose to join within this five-year period, your accumulated weeks of credit will expire, your registration fee will be forfeited, and you will not receive the credit toward a future initiation fee.

JOINING EQUITY

When you wish to join Equity, you must complete the membership application and pay the then-current initiation fee. Your $100 EMC registration fee will be credited against your initiation fee (except as noted above). Once you join Equity, you will also be subject to basic dues and working dues. Call Equity or visit www.actorsequity.org for current rates.

IMPORTANT NOTES

- It is your responsibility to keep your contact information with Equity's Membership Department.

- Equity policy does not permit the duplication of names among its members. Be aware that the name you use as a Membership Candidate may not be available when you become eligible to join Equity.

- There are no established salaries for Membership Candidates except those agreed upon by you and the producer who employs you.

- The EMC Program is not available to Non-resident Aliens.

- The 40 week EMC exam was discontinued by Equity's Council on November 20, 2001. Permission to take the exam may be grandfathered for individuals who joined the EMC Program prior to February 15, 2003, upon written request to the EMC department at the nearest Equity regional office.

- EMC policies and procedures are subject to change. Please contact Equity's website for updates.

Please contact the nearest Equity office with questions or concerns regarding the EMC program.

Glossary

Academy Players Directory: Publication that contains actors' photos and lists agents who represent them. The directory is published three times a year. An actor must be a member of one of the acting unions in order to be listed in the directory.

Actors' Equity Association (AEA) (www.actorsequity.org): Also known as "Equity." Equity is the union which has jurisdiction over stage performers and stage managers.

Actor's Routine: "Illness" an actor might acquire after an audition: "I should have . . . . , I could have . . . . , Why didn't I . . . . ?"

Age Range: Ages that an actor can possibly play. This range can, but doesn't necessarily have to, include the actor's real age. It is *not* recommended to put an "age range" on a resume.

Agent: Person who represents the actor. The agent is responsible for getting the actor on auditions and interviews (one and the same), and for negotiating the actor's contracts with employers.

American Federation of Television and Radio Artists (AFTRA) (www.aftra.org): Union which includes jurisdiction over performers in live and taped TV shows (newscasters and announcers included), taped commercials, radio shows, phonograph records, educational media, CD games, etc.

Association of Talent Agents (ATA): Nonprofit organization which represents talent agents.

Audition: Also known as "interview." Meeting with agent, casting director, director, et al., at which an actor usually reads for a role.

Backstage / Backstage West (www.backstage.com): Show business magazine published weekly in New York and Los Angeles, respectively. It lists casting calls and other general information of interest to the actor.

Billing: Credit line attached to the actor's name for a particular role ("Star," "Guest Star," "Featuring," "Introducing," etc.).

Breakdown Services: A publication with editions in Los Angeles, New York, Vancouver, Toronto, and London, that lists roles being cast for TV/film/commercials. It is distributed daily (except weekends) to managers and agents.

Callback: A return audition/interview to be seen again.

Casting Director: Person who screens actors who will potentially meet the director and/or producer for casting.

Chicago Area Theatre (CAT): Equity theatres and contracts in the Chicago area. CAT contracts generally have lower wage minimums because of their smaller houses.

Client: From an actor's point of view, the term generally refers to the actor in his relationship with the agent. The relationship is often referred to as the "agent/client" relationship. In commercial work, "client" generally refers to the advertiser sponsoring the commercial. In TV and film work, it generally refers to whoever is paying for the project.

Cold Reading: Type of reading for which the actor is given very little, if any, rehearsal time in the interview before performing the material. Most TV, film, and commercial auditions include a cold reading.

Composite: Group of photos arranged on an 8½ x 11 sheet of lithograph paper that shows the actor or model in different situations. In the larger markets of Los Angeles and New York they are out of favor for actors and not presently being used. However, models and stuntmen still use them. Composites are sometimes used by actors in the smaller markets.

Council of Resident Stock Theatres (CORST): Negotiating body for Equity resident dramatic stock companies all over the country. To be considered a stock company the theatre must be producing two or more plays simultaneously. The main difference between CORST and COST is that COST is a non-resident company and CORST is a resident company (i.e., maintains a nucleus of players from one play to the next).

Council of Stock Theatres (COST): Negotiating body for non-resident Equity theatres all over the country.

Cover Letter: Letter sent along with an actor's package (i.e., photo and resume) to agents, casting directors, directors, etc.

Disney World/Orlando Contract: Actor's Equity Association contract for performers at Disney World in Orlando, Florida.

Equity: See Actors' Equity Association.

Extra: Also know as "background player." In TV and film work, a player who doesn't speak any lines of dialogue; generally referred to as "background" or "atmosphere" work. In commercial work, however, such an actor might be considered a principal player (not an extra) whether he speaks a line or not. If the actor is on-camera and is identified with the product, demonstrates the product, reacts to the message in the commercial, or performs a stunt he might be considered a principal player without mouthing a word. The determination can become touchy, and often SAG has to view the commercial to decide who is a principal and who is an extra.

Freelancing: Refers to an actor representing himself instead of having agent representation.

General Interview: Interview in which an actor might just talk to a casting director, director, producer, etc. The interviewer might not even be casting any particular project at that moment. It's a get-acquainted type of meeting that could lead to auditions for specific projects in the future.

Headshot: An 8 x 10 photo that is used by most actors. The photo is usually taken from the middle of the bust line or shoulders up.

Holding Fee: In commercials, fee that is given to an actor even though his commercial isn't presently airing. The fee is compensation for the fact that the actor can't perform in any other commercials for any product that competes with the original product during a specified period of time.

Hollywood Area Theatre/Bay Area Theatre (HAT/BAT): Type of Equity theatre contract used for the Hollywood and San Francisco areas, respectively. These contracts generally have lower wage minimums for the actors due to their smaller audiences.

Hollywood Reporter (www.hollywoodreporter.com): Show business magazine published daily (excluding weekends) in Hollywood. It is distributed in many areas, but its primary concern is with Hollywood. Though it's basically a business magazine for the entertainment industry, it often includes casting news of interest to the actor.

Interview: In the screen world, refers to auditions for TV, film, and commercial roles. In stage acting, refers to a meeting between the actor and the people responsible for casting a production. It is a get-acquainted session where the actor brings his photo and resume and chats with the personnel holding the audition.

L.A. 99 Seat Plan: Term used for stage productions in Los Angeles for which the theatre has "99 seats or less," and the actors don't get paid. These plays are showcase plays for the actor and do come under Equity's jurisdiction. Both Equity and non-Equity members may perform in such plays. Formerly, these plays were referred to as "Equity Waiver" plays.

League of Resident Theatres (LORT): Negotiating body for Equity resident theatres all over the country. To be considered a resident the atre the theatre must be producing a series of plays. The difference between LORT theatres and other resident theatres is that LORT theatres are non-profit organizations.

Letter of Agreement (LOA): Type of Equity contract used by developing theatres. Equity has an individual agreement with each theatre based on the specific situation of that theatre. There is no standard contract here. Different minimum and maximum pay scales are used for each situation.

Manager: Person who represents the actor but who isn't affiliated or franchised by the unions/associations and is *not* considered an agent. The manager operates more in a managing capacity than in a negotiating capacity. His fee is usually anywhere from 10 to 20 percent (fifteen percent being the norm) of the actor's salary, but there are no limits.

Matching: With regards to auditions, refers to "physically" being right for a part. If the director were casting, for example, roles for a family, then the family would have to "match" each other. This term is used more for TV, film, and commercials than for stage.

Monologue: Dramatic sketch given by one actor alone. Generally a monologue is used for stage auditions rather than for screen interviews.

National Association of Talent Representatives (NATR): Nonprofit organization which represents talent agents.

Network Approval: Refers to a television network approving a certain actor for a certain role being handled by its studio. Network approval is usually only needed for a few of the major roles.

Non-Equity: Type of play production, which is not produced under an Equity contract. Equity members may not participate in this type of production.

Non-SAG: Type of film, commercial, or filmed TV production that isn't under the jurisdiction of the Screen Actors Guild. Members of SAG may not participate in this type of production.

Off-Broadway (in reference to Equity contracts): Type of Equity contract used for Off-Broadway theatres in New York. These contracts usually have lower wage minimums because of the smaller houses in the Off-Broadway market.

Off-Off Broadway (in reference to Equity contracts): Any production in New York City that is not Broadway or Off-Broadway. Basically Off-Off Broadway refers to any production in New York City that is completely non-Equity. Equity members may not perform in typical Off-Off Broadway productions.

Package: Term used to describe an actor's photo and resume.

Padding: Adding irrelevant, unimportant, or inaccurate information to a resume to make it look more impressive. This is a no-no for actors.

Principal Player: Under SAG jurisdiction, anyone who speaks a line of dialogue on or off camera, or anyone who performs a stunt. Under AFTRA jurisdiction, anyone who speaks a line of dialogue if he is in a situation comedy, or anyone who speaks over five lines if he's in a variety show or daytime serial. In commercials, under both unions, anyone who speaks a line of dialogue, or anyone whose face appears while demonstrating or illustrating the product, or anyone whose face is shown reacting to the message in the commercial, or someone who performs a stunt.

Principal Role: Role that falls into the category described in "Principal Player."

Producer: In television, individual(s) totally responsible to the network for the finished product of the show. In film and stage, the producer is totally responsible to the backers for the finished product. The producer is in charge of hiring the director and crew. He handles the financial responsibilities as well.

Product Conflict: In commercials, it would mean that the actor has two commercials airing, or for which he's being held, and the products compete with each other in the marketplace.

Production Contract: Standard contract used for any single Equity production. The Production Contract has the highest-paying minimum contract for the actor.

Residual: A payment to the actor for each re-airing of a TV show after the initial airing. Although people use "residuals" when it comes to commercials, technically they are called "use fees."

Rounds: Refers to stage actors dropping off their photos and resumes at casting directors', directors', or producers' offices. Term generally used in New York more so than in other cities. Also refers to agents meeting with casting directors and directors regarding their clients.

Screen Actors Guild (SAG): Union for actors which has jurisdiction over films, filmed TV shows, and filmed commercials.

Showcase Code: Agreement used for showcase plays in New York for Off-Off Broadway theatres, which have "99 seats or less." Any actor, Equity or non-Equity, may audition for these plays.

Sides: Term used for the few pages an actor reads in an audition.

Sign-In Sheet: With regards to auditions, refers to the sheet of paper each actor signs as he enters an audition. The actor signs his name, his agent's name and phone number, his own Social Security number or union membership number, the time he arrives for the interview, and the time he leaves the interview. Because of security reasons, SAG will permit the actor to use his SAG member number instead of his social security number.

Slating: The stating of an actor's name and sometimes the additional stating of the name of the agent who represents him, on camera, during an audition.

Small Professional Theatre Contract (SPTC): Contract used for theatres with a seating capacity of 349 seats or less in cities outside of New York, San Francisco, and Los Angeles county. Pay levels are tied to box office potential and generally have low minimums.

Submit (Submission): Term referring to the sending out of a photo and resume by an agent or individual to a casting director, director, or producer, in hopes of getting the actor an interview.

Taft-Hartley: Federal law stating that a person can work a certain amount of time on a union job without having to join that union. As it typically applies to the acting unions, an actor can work up to 30 *calendar* days on his first job without joining the appropriate union. However, on his second job, or any job that lasts over 30 calendar days, he must join if he wants to work on a show under that particular union. This law does not apply in right-to-work states.

Test Market: In reference to commercials, the testing of a commercial in front of an audience to see what types of responses the commercial receives from that audience.

Theatre for Young Audiences (TYA): Type of Equity contract used for children's plays. The plays usually are performed in the daylight hours and aren't over an hour-and-a-half in length.

Type: Refers to physical characteristics of the actor. A director might want, for example, an "all-American" type.

Under Five: Under an AFTRA contract, an actor who has a speaking role of five lines or fewer.

Unsolicited: Usually refers to material (photo and resume) sent directly to an industry professional by an actor rather than by an agent.

Use-Fee: A repayment to the actor for each re-airing of his commercial. For television and films such re-airing payments are referred to as "residuals."

Variety: Show business magazine published weekly and daily (two different versions). The weekly is an international issue published in New York, while the daily is published in Hollywood and is primarily for the Hollywood area. Though they are both basically business magazines, they do include some production and casting news.

Voice-Over: Type of work in which the actor isn't seen, but his voice is heard.

Western Civic Light Opera (WCLO): Actors' Equity Association contract used for Western region, community nonprofit musical theatres.

Wrap: Refers to the ending of the shooting day. Used more in TV, film, and commercial shooting than in stage work.

Abbreviations

AEA: Actors' Equity Association (also known as "Equity")
AFTRA: American Federation of Television and Radio Artists
AGMA: American Guild of Musical Artists
AGVA: American Guild of Variety Artists
ATA: Association of Talent Agents
CAT: Chicago Area Theatre
CORST: Council of Resident Stock Theatres
COST: Council of Stock Theatres
HAT/BAT: Hollywood Area Theatre/Bay Area Theatre
LORT: League of Resident Theatres
NATR: National Association of Talent Representatives
SAG: Screen Actors Guild
SPTC: Small Professional Theatre Contract
TYA: Theatre for Young Audiences
WCLO: Western Civic Light Opera

About The Author

TOM LOGAN is a member of the Directors Guild of America, the Screen Actors Guild, the American Federation of Television and Radio Artists, and Actors' Equity Association.

His feature film directing credits include: *Dream Trap* (which he also wrote), *Escape From Cuba* (which he also co-wrote), *Shakma*, *The Night Brings Charlie*, *Shoot*, *Kings Ransom*, and *Smooth Operator*. All of these films are in worldwide release.

He has directed many television shows and hundreds of national/international commercials. His television pilot directing credits (all of which have sold) include: *Modern Miracles* (which he also wrote), *The Neon Tiki Tribe* (children's TV show, which he also wrote), *Working Title* for the CBC (which he also produced), and the nationally syndicated children's TV shows: *What If* and *Kid Town Hall*. Early in his directing career he wrote, produced, and directed many episodes of the number one-rated, nationally syndicated TV show, *Real Stories of the Highway Patrol*. He has also directed many episodes of the very popular TV series, BloodHounds, Inc., which stars Richard Thomas.

He has won two New Discovery Awards: 1996 Best Director award for "Outstanding Achievement in Direction" for his film *Escape From Cuba*, and the 1995 Producers' Choice award for "Outstanding

Direction of a Television Variety Program" for a live telecast of the 1995 Miss North America Pageant. He is also the winner of the Golden Halo award for the "Most Outstanding Contribution to the Entertainment Industry" for his contributions made as an acting instructor for the studios and for his acting seminars. In addition, he won the Bronze Halo award for "Outstanding Contribution to the Entertainment Industry" for authoring two top-selling books. Both awards are given annually by the Southern California Motion Picture Council.

Tom no longer acts, but prior to becoming a full-time screen director he starred, co-starred, or guest starred in hundreds of prime time TV series, feature films, live stage productions from New York to Los Angeles, and in over one hundred national commercials. In addition, he has had recurring roles on three network soap operas, including on and off General Hospital for twelve years.

Early in his career, he was an acting coach for the studios, whose clients included top stars from all three major networks, Academy Award winners, top baseball and football players, rock stars, and other well-known celebrities. In Los Angeles he simultaneously headed the TV/film acting departments at two of the world's most prestigious acting schools—The American Academy of Dramatic Arts/West (1981-89) and the American Film Institute (1980-89).

He has performed his award-winning acting seminars in five countries and 47 states, mostly for the same clients for the past 25 years. He holds a B.A. (cum laude, Honor Roll, Dean's List) in Theatre Arts from California State University.

Tom holds the highest airplane pilot rating one can obtain from the FAA—Airline Transport Pilot. He owns a Piper Arrow and is an instrument-rated commercial pilot who, although he doesn't have time to teach flying, holds all instructor ratings one can obtain from the FAA—CFI, CFII, MEI, BGI, AGI.

Tom has two sons and lives in southern California.